Coleman

The OUTDOOR ADVENTURE Cookbook

Coleman ® *EXPERT ADVICE* ⛺ *CAMPSITE TIPS* ❄ *GEAR GUIDE*

The OUTDOOR ADVENTURE *Cookbook*

THE OFFICIAL COOKBOOK
FROM THE ULTIMATE CAMPING AUTHORITY

Oxmoor House®

©2017 Time Inc. Books

Published by Oxmoor House, an imprint of Time Inc. Books
225 Liberty Street, New York, NY 10281

Editors: Meredith Butcher, Rachel Quinlivan West
Senior Manager, Business Development + Partnerships: Nina Reed
Project Editor: Melissa Brown
Writer: Lisa Trottier
Designer: Liane Burns
Junior Designer: AnnaMaria Jacob
Photographers: Iain Bagwell, Caitlin Bensel, Jen Causey,
    Lisa Corson, Rob Culpepper, Greg Dupree, Alison Miksch,
    Colin Price, Victor Protasio, Becky Stayner
Prop Stylists: Mary Clayton Carl, Kay E. Clarke, Missie Crawford,
    Thom Driver, Paige Hicks, Lindsey Lower, Katherine Tucker
Food Stylists: Torie Cox, Margaret Monroe Dickey,
    Kellie Gerber Kelley, Erin Merhar, Tori Prendergast,
    Karen Rankin, Catherine Crowell Steele
Recipe Developers and Testers: Robin Bashinsky, Mark Driskill,
    Paige Grandjean, Adam Hickman, Julia Levy, Pam Lolley,
    Robby Melvin, Callie Nash, Marianne Williams, Deb Wise
Assistant Production Director: Sue Chodakiewicz
Senior Production Manager: Greg A. Amason
Copy Editors: Jacqueline Giovanelli, Jasmine Hodges
Proofreader: Rebecca Brennan
Indexer: Mary Ann Laurens
Fellows: Helena Joseph, Hailey Middlebrook, Kyle Grace Mills

Text and photos, pages 6, 9, 11, 13 (equipment), 17, 18, 25, 26, 28:
Used under license from Coleman.

Special thanks to Doug and Susan Wagner

ISBN-13: 978-0-8487-5139-5
Library of Congress Control Number: 2016962645

First Edition 2017

Printed in the United States of America

10 9 8 7 6 5 4 3 2 1

We welcome your comments and suggestions about
Time Inc. Books.
Please write to us at:
Time Inc. Books
Attention: Book Editors
P.O. Box 62310
Tampa, Florida 33662-2310

Time Inc. Books products may be purchased for business or
promotional use. For information on bulk purchases, please
contact Christi Crowley in the Special Sales Department
at (845) 895-9858.

Contents

CHAPTER ONE

BREAKFAST 30

CHAPTER TWO

DRINKS, SNACKS & APPS 66

CHAPTER THREE

SANDWICHES & SALADS 100

CHAPTER FOUR

HOT MAINS 152

CHAPTER FIVE

SIDE DISHES 206

CHAPTER SIX

DESSERTS 236

≋ INTRODUCTION ≋

WHEN CAMPING, the meal is the thing. No one has an appointment to run off to, and there's certainly nothing on TV. This is it: The scenery around you and a snapping, flickering fire are all the entertainment you need. Friends and family pull off their hiking boots, slip on their flip-flops, and gather around the fire and the food in an elemental pull that hasn't changed since the Ice Age. This is a moment of undistracted togetherness that is hard to come by in the swirl of daily life. Enjoy it.

Keep in mind that cooking outside slows you down a bit. No one ever said that it's a super-efficient way to get a meal together. But that's part of the point. And, after all, what else do you have planned for these late afternoon into early evening hours? Take your time, letting the evening unspool as the sounds of chopping and sizzling blend with the shouts of kids running free, and the smells from bubbling pots mix with the fresh scent of pine needles.

No question, cooking without your fridge, your oven, your kitchen sink takes a bit of a rethink. There are hard-fought lessons to be learned (look for Think Like a Scout tips throughout this book). It can be a bit unpredictable. Sparks fly—literally. But with some sound advice, a couple of key pans, and some careful prep and packing, it can absolutely be done. There's no need to fall back on canned chili. And if the chipmunks run off with your croutons or the fire refuses to cook evenly, think of it this way: You'll never have a more appreciative audience than a crowd of campers. After a big day outside, they'll be ravenous, and grateful for the meal you can conjure from the fire. Whip up something delicious and nourishing, and you'll be a hero.

THE COLEMAN® STORY

W.C. Coleman could see the light for the darkness. The young salesman was taking a stroll after a hard day's work selling typewriters, and spotted a new type of lamplight in a drugstore window in Brockton, Alabama. This new light burned with a strong, steady, white flame and was fueled by gasoline. The standard lamp of the era burned kerosene and produced a smoky, flickering, yellowish light. W.C. had very poor eyesight, and was keenly interested in this new, steady, white light that enabled him to read even the smallest print in books and on medicine bottles. Coleman saw potential in the new light, and through his vision a new company was born that would eventually make his name synonymous with outdoor fun.

[1900 – 1929]

FIRST LIGHT

In 1905, W.C. Coleman wanted to demonstrate just what his new gas lamps were capable of. He strung his lamps from poles on both sides of the football field at Fairmount College in Wichita, Kansas. According to Coleman historians, the first night football game west of the Mississippi occurred that evening under Coleman gas lights and resulted in a 24–0 shutout of Cooper College by the Fairmount College Wheatshockers.

At the turn of the century in America, electric service was not an option in rural parts of the country. When the sun went down, the workday ended. In 1909, W.C. Coleman started selling a portable table lamp that would become a staple in rural homes, and five years later introduced a product that would help transform the company from a local concern into a national necessity. The new 300 candlepower lantern provided working light in every direction for 100 yards and could light the far corners of a barn. The lantern lengthened the time farmers and ranchers could work, significantly boosting productivity and fundamentally changing rural America. It wasn't just for civilians either, as the US government declared this lantern an "essential item" for the troops serving in World War I, and nearly 70,000 lanterns were distributed to American forces fighting in Europe.

[1930 – 1945]

ESSENTIAL EQUIPMENT

During World War II, like many companies, The Coleman Company did its part to support the war effort. In June 1942, the Army Quartermaster Corps issued an urgent request to Coleman: Field troops were in dire need of a compact stove that could operate within a wide range of conditions in multiple theaters, weighed less than 5 pounds, could be no larger than a quart bottle of milk, and could burn any kind of fuel. And, the US Army wanted 5,000 of the stoves delivered in 60 days.

Work commenced immediately, and the end product far exceeded anything the army had requested: The stove could work at 60° below and up to 150° above Fahrenheit, burn all kinds of fuel, weighed just 3¹⁄₂ pounds, and was smaller than a quart bottle of milk. The first order for 5,000 units was flown to US forces involved in Operation Torch, an allied invasion of North Africa in 1942. World War II journalist Ernie Pyle devoted 15 news articles to the Coleman® pocket stove and considered it one of the two most important pieces of noncombat equipment in the war effort, the other being the Jeep.

[1946 – 1953]

HAVE COLEMAN, WILL TRAVEL

When the war ended, Coleman's business boomed. American families had money, a new interstate highway system, and fancy new cars. With this newfound mobility came the urge to travel and

explore. Roadways were improving, but hotels in those days weren't on every corner. Instead, vacationers simply pulled off the road and made camp. Along with the lantern, the camping stove made an ideal traveling companion and was a must-have for family getaways.

[1954 – 1999]
ON THE BUBBLE

In 1954, coolers were made of steel, which would sweat, rust, and were generally inefficient. A Coleman engineer saw a child blowing soap bubbles and came up with a new cooler concept: a plastic "bubble" was formed out of heated sheet plastic, molded into the shape needed for the cooler, and then snapped into place. This groundbreaking process revolutionized the cooler industry in 1957, making the Coleman cooler lighter, more efficient, and easier to clean than any other coolers at this time. This process is essentially the same one that's been used ever since.

In the decades that followed, Coleman adapted to the changes and trends in outdoor recreation. In 1962, it added tents and sleeping bags to its outdoor line. Coleman battery lighting hit the market in the '80s. The '90s saw an even more comprehensive catalog of Coleman products, such as camping furniture and accessories, along with award-winning backpacking stoves with innovative fuel systems.

[21ST CENTURY]
A BIG TENT

In the 21st century, Coleman has added many recognizable brands to its family of goods. Under the Coleman tent, you'll now find Sevylor® floats and towables, Stearns® life vests, MadDog Gear® ATV accessories, and AeroBed® airbeds.

What started out as a lamp that could light up four corners of a barn has become a company that has helped light all four corners of the globe. Coleman products have journeyed deep in the Sahara Desert and been along on treks all the way to the South Pole. Coleman lanterns guided aircraft to safe landings in the Andes Mountains in South America in the 1920s, and helped climbers reach the top of Mt. Everest in the next century. Hiking, camping, fishing, hunting, boating, swimming, four-wheeling, relaxing, tailgating: Being in the outdoors has so much to offer, and Coleman has everything to help you get out there.

PACK FOR CAMPING

The first camping trip takes the most legwork as you pull together gear you may not have on hand. After that, if you keep your camping kit more or less together in dedicated boxes or bins, it becomes much easier and quicker to pack. It's helpful to create a packing list that's customized to your climate, your family, and your interests. Keep it on your phone or computer so you can tweak it for each trip and check off items as you pack. If you're camping with several families, a list also makes it easy to divvy up some items so not everyone needs to bring a camping stove and a lantern, for example.

Here's a starter packing list that you can customize for your own trip:

FOR SLEEPING
- ❑ Tent, rain fly, and stakes
- ❊ **TIP:** Bringing one that's designed for two more people than you have leaves room for clothes at the sides and helps keep things organized.
- ❑ Small hammer for pounding in stakes (a rock will also do the trick)
- ❑ A tarp for under the tent (many tents come with one that fits perfectly)
- ❑ Sleeping pads (extra blankets/comforters will do in a pinch)
- ❑ Sleeping bags
- ❑ Pillows
- ❊ **TIP:** If you're tight on space, you can just roll up a fleece or down jacket and use it as a pillow.
- ❑ Earplugs (in case of snoring tentmates or off-tune neighbors)

FOR THE SITE
- ❑ Folding chairs
- ❑ A length of rope for a clothesline
- ❑ A lantern (propane-powered for the table and/or battery-powered for the tent)
- ❑ Flashlights or headlamps (headlamps can be handier when trying to clean up or brush your teeth in the dark)
- ❑ Extra batteries

FOR THE FIRE
- ❑ Matches/lighter
- ❑ Fire starters, either store-bought or DIY (page 22)
- ❑ Charcoal
- ❑ Saw or ax
- ❑ Wood (if allowed to bring in)

FOR ADVENTURES
- ❑ Day pack/s
- ❑ Canteens/water bottles
- ❑ Swimsuits/water shoes
- ❑ Field guides to plants/birds
- ❑ Star chart
- ❑ Binoculars
- ❑ Map
- ❊ **TIP:** Yes, you'll have your phone with you, but it may not get a signal, or may run out of power.

FOR COOKING
- ❊ **TIP:** It is easiest to keep essentials in their own bin. Or, even better, a bin of tools and a bin of food.
- ❑ Stove and fuel
- ❑ Cooler(s)
- ❑ Ice
- ❑ Nonbreakable plates, bowls, cups, utensils
- ❑ A folding table for extra work space, if you have one
- ❑ Tablecloth (oilcloth is easy to wipe down)
- ❑ Cutting board
- ❑ Good chopping knife and paring knife
- ❑ Coffeemaker (page 49)
- ❑ 10-inch cast-iron skillet
- ❑ 12-inch cast-iron skillet
- ❑ 7½-quart cast-iron Dutch oven (also handy for heating water for cleaning dishes)
- ❑ Cast-iron griddle
- ❑ Spatula
- ❑ Wooden spoon
- ❑ Hot pads/oven mitts
- ❑ Measuring cups and spoons
- ❑ Bottle opener/wine opener
- ❑ Can opener
- ❑ Aluminum foil
- ❑ Paper towels
- ❑ Dish towels
- ❑ Resealable storage bags
- ❑ Trash bags
- ❑ Biodegradable dish soap
- ❑ Sponge/scrubber
- ❑ Cooking oil
- ❑ Olive oil
- ❑ Salt and pepper

CLOTHING
Other than the expected scruffy clothing to fit the climate and plan, bring along:
- ❑ Sun hat
- ❑ Flip-flops or other slip-on shoes
- ❑ Sturdy hiking/adventure shoes
- ❑ Warm socks
- ❑ Long underwear or sweats
- ❑ Warm jacket
- ❑ Warm hat

TOILETRIES
- ❑ Sunscreen
- ❑ Bug spray
- ❑ Biodegradable hand soap
- ❑ Towel (keep separate from your beach/lake towels to avoid a damp, sandy dry-off)
- ❑ Baby wipes

JUST IN CASE
- ❑ Pocketknife
- ❑ A tarp or two and some nylon rope or bungee cords, for improvising extra shelter
- ❑ A rain jacket
- ❑ First Aid Kit
- ❑ A compass
- ❑ Roll of toilet paper

PANTRY
You'll build your food list from the recipes you choose, but some must-haves to bring along are:
- ❑ Ground coffee/tea/cocoa
- ❑ Butter
- ❑ Cooking oil/olive oil
- ❑ Cooking spray
- ❑ Salt/pepper

FOR FUN
- ❑ Bikes/scooters
- ❑ Mitts/balls/Frisbees
- ❑ Playing cards/board games
- ❑ Water toys
- ❑ Glow sticks for after dark
- ❑ Sidewalk chalk
- ❑ Beach towels

IF YOU'RE BACKPACKING ...

You'll hear people use the words "camping" and "backpacking" interchangeably, but when it comes to gear, backpacking is a very different challenge. The primary considerations when heading into the backcountry are:

BULK. A tent and sleeping bag can easily fill a large pack if you don't choose wisely. Everything you pack will need to be considered on its merits per square inch. Regular backpackers spend top dollar to shave off a few inches here, a few there. Others simply go minimalist, bringing the bare minimum of what they have. (Say hello to your pan/cereal bowl/Frisbee/dishwashing tub!)

WEIGHT. A pack that feels fine when you try it on in your living room can quickly become your worst enemy a few miles up the trail. (See Bill Bryson's *A Walk in the Woods* for more on this.) A bottle of wine or an extra pair of hiking shoes can become an unimaginable luxury when packing for weight.

WATER. With no water on tap in the backcountry, a good, high-volume filter becomes an essential tool. Bring along a low-volume one and you may spend half the day filtering lake water, drop-by-drop.

WARMTH. You'll need to balance your efforts to minimize weight and bulk with your need to stay warm under changing conditions far from the nearest store or structure. A shivering night is no fun. You don't need a lot of warm clothes, but you do need some good ones.

BEARS. If you're in bear country, you'll need to keep food and toiletries in a plastic bear can or hang anything that smells good (including toothpaste, wipes, sunscreen) from a high tree branch. If you plan to use a can, test-pack it at least a day in advance. If the food you don't plan to eat the first evening won't fit in the can, better to make adjustments while you're still near a store.

HANDY PACKING TIPS

TIP: A worthwhile splurge if you have the space is an extra folding table. No one ever complained about having too much surface space to work on while cooking at a campsite! Coleman has a handful of options that fold up snugly and take up minimal space in your car. You'll just want to put it into the car at bedtime if the night will be damp.

TIP: If you have pots and pans you use just for camping, the next time you open a new pair of shoes, don't toss the little silica packets buried in the tissue paper. Instead store them with your camping pans. It guards against rust during the months your pots are socked away in your basement or garage.

How to
PACK A COOLER

A WELL-PACKED COOLER WILL MAKE COOKING SO MUCH EASIER. SOME LESSONS WE'VE LEARNED SO YOU DON'T HAVE TO:

CHOOSE THE RIGHT COOLER

Coolers are typically rated on how many days they can keep contents cool (in ideal conditions). For camping trips of three or more days, you want to select a cooler that has a greater amount of high-quality insulation (look for insulation in the lid, as well). For day use, a less-insulated cooler might be sufficient. Choose one that is consistent with your usage, and you'll be setting yourself up for success.

CHOOSE YOUR ICE WISELY

Block ice lasts longer than cubed, but cubed can be poured into the cracks between food. A mix of the two works best. (When purchasing ice, the ideal guideline is using .75 lb. of ice for each quart in your cooler.) Consider freezing plastic bottles of water to use as block ice. When they melt, they won't soak everything, and you'll have cool water to drink.

TURN YOUR FOOD INTO A COLD PACK

Aside from foods you'll use the first day and any delicate foods, freeze anything and everything you can before packing the cooler. Jugs of water or lemonade become ice blocks, as do packets of bacon, sauces, bags of chili … you get the idea. Anything that can't be frozen should be prechilled.

NOTE: **Glass containers and stainless water bottles are the exception—they do NOT freeze well.**

CONSIDER THE ORDER

The order you put your food in the cooler is important. Start at the bottom of the cooler with the most perishable foods, such as meat and dairy, and work up with items that are less of a concern. Layer ice in between items. Keep meat away from the edges, which will get warmer in the sun, and keep produce on top of the ice.

START WITH A CLEAN SLATE

A cooler should be cleaned and dried between uses. If raw meat was stored (and potentially leaked) in the cooler, you should disinfect it with a diluted bleach solution prior to storing it. If you have only used the cooler for beverages, hot soapy water is sufficient. Regardless of what has been stored in the cooler, a person's hands can introduce soil and bacteria, so it's smart to give it a good cleaning after each use.

PRECHILL YOUR COOLER

If you're worried about your ice making it to the finish line, get a head start by filling the cooler with ice water for a couple of hours just before packing it.

LEAKPROOF EVERYTHING

Milky ice water is nasty. So is slimy cheese. Put everything in leakproof containers, and when in doubt, double-bag it. Be sure to test them—many containers do not have leakproof seals.

YOUR SECRET WEAPON: ADDITIONAL COOLERS

If you're traveling with a big crew or staying more than a couple of nights, cooler space is likely to be at a premium. Additional coolers can save the day. It works better if you give each a specific job.

BEVERAGES ARE BULKY

Packing a separate cooler for drinks will help keep the food coolers cold longer since they won't be opened as often.

PACK A COOLER FOR EACH DAY

For multi-day trips (and if you have the room), consider packing a cooler for each day to keep food cold until you're ready to use it.

MOVE YOUR COOLERS

Throughout the duration of your trip, move coolers around your site to keep them out of the sun. Temperatures can be many degrees cooler in the shade.

⇒ MORE PACKING TIPS ⇐

HOW TO KEEP THINGS ORGANIZED

YOU'LL BE PACKING A LOT OF GEAR FOR YOUR TRIP.
Think in categories. Hunting for every last thing you need takes the fun out of camping. It will be easier to keep things organized at the campsite if your kitchen tools are in one bin, your beach toys in a bag, your toiletries and towels all together.

AS YOU PACK, TAKE A LOOK AT GEAR THAT'S BEEN SITTING IN THE GARAGE FOR A LONG TIME— better to discover at home that you're missing several tent stakes or a mouse has taken up residence in your camp stove. If it's been awhile since you've been camping, fire up the stove and lantern to make sure they're still working.

PACK A SEPARATE BAG OF CLOTHES FOR EACH CAMPER. This will mean less digging through clothes in the tent. Hard suitcases are too bulky for a tent—pack each person's clothes into a different colored duffel for an easy ID. An open bin will work well, too, since you'll only be carrying the clothes from the car to the tent. A mesh cylindrical bin makes it easier to dig for those warm socks on a chilly evening.

BRING ALONG ONE LARGE EMPTY DUFFEL OR CLEAN TRASH BAG for everyone to stuff their dirty clothes into. This will keep the tent more organized and fresh clothes fresher.

TRY TO PACK THE CAR so that the first things you'll need on arrival are the last to go in; This makes the unpacking and setting up camp more orderly. So, the tent should be easy to reach when the car is packed.

FINALLY, PUT SOME ESSENTIALS ON THE TOP OF THE PILE. Keep a lantern, headlamps, spare batteries, and insect repellent handy so that when you arrive at the site, you have them if you need them.

IF YOU'RE BRINGING THE KIDS

GET THE KIDS ON BOARD. Older kids can pack their own clothes from a list. Younger ones can choose and add a stuffed animal and a book to their bag. Make sure they bring anything they need to get through the night happily, or you and all your campground neighbors will be sorry. (Pack some earplugs just in case.)

DO A DRY RUN AT HOME. If you haven't camped in a while, shake out and set up your gear at home. Seeing the tent come together in the living room or the back-yard, and spending an afternoon or a night in it, makes kids feel comfier with the idea of camping and helps get them excited for the adventure. It's a chance for you to show them where to keep their clothes, how to turn on their headlamp, and run over rules like No Sandy Feet in the Tent. It also points out any flaws in your gear or your packing list while you're still near a store.

PACK FOR FUN. Kids love the freedom that camping brings. Make the most of it by bringing simple outdoor toys they can enjoy with their siblings or buddies. Sidewalk chalk will turn your pull-in into a work of art. Frisbees will get hours of use. And magnifying glasses and field guides will turn your kids into explorers. If you have room, most car campgrounds are ideal places to ride bikes and scooters, and the kids will love roaming the loops in a pack. (Note, helmets are required in many parks.) After dark, glowing light sticks make miniature light sabers or batons (and, as a bonus, they also make the kids a lot easier to track down when it's time for bed).

REVIEW THE RULES. Point out any areas that have been designated off-limits, make sure the kids know not to roam right through other people's campsites, and introduce them to the concept of quiet hours. Point out any hazards—poison oak, deep or fast water—to all the kids, even seasoned campers.

☀ **TIP:** If you have any of those interlocking foam floor pads made for kids' rooms, bring them along and put them together in the tent for a cheery, supercozy layer that will also ward off the chill.

PLAN FOR MEALS

Meal planning is a key part of making your campsite culinary experience a good one. Being organized from the start can help keep things simple once you get to your location and make on-site meal preparation significantly easier. Follow these tips to set yourself up for a wonderful outdoor experience.

MAKE A GAME PLAN. Begin by marking the recipes in this book that most appeal to you. Create a grid of the meals you'll need for the duration of your trip: **DAY 1:** lunch, dinner. **DAY 2:** breakfast, lunch, dinner. And so on. Start jotting meals into the grid, slotting recipes that use the most perishable ingredients (strawberries, tomatoes, salad greens, fresh baguette) first, those made up of hardier or shelf-stable ingredients (citrus, cabbage, tortillas, pita) later.

DIVVY IT UP. If you're traveling with a whole crew of people, it can make things more fun and less work if everyone works together. Some like to alternate dinner duty and leave everyone to prep their own breakfasts and lunches. Others put one family in charge of breakfast, another in charge of a portable lunch, another in charge of dinner, maybe even another family—less skilled at cooking—in charge of dishes. To make things more interesting, you could make dinner a friendly competition to encourage people to up their game.

Handy Tip

BRING AN EASY PLAN B [OR TWO]

Even if you have a full schedule of great meals planned, it's a good idea to bring an easy fallback: spaghetti and premade sauce, soup from the prepared section at the grocery store, or anything else that can be whipped up in no time. That way, if it starts raining, or you fail to catch that trout you're counting on, or the fire is being stubborn, you won't need to stress.

PREP AS MUCH AS POSSIBLE AT HOME

Prep work done at home pays off big at the campsite. It decreases the bulk of the food you need to bring, makes ingredients more organized and easier to locate and use, and helps meals come together quickly—all of which leaves you more time for lounging by the fire or enjoying the view with a cocktail. In general, we like to smooth the way for campground cooking by prepping the following:

Make any **MARINADES** and put in a sealable bag with the **MEAT.** Freeze before packing the cooler.

Premeasure any **DRY MIXES**—for breads, pancakes, etc. Pancake mix kept in a resealable bag can get a dose of milk at the site and be mixed right in the bag. Snip off one corner and squeeze dollops of batter right onto the griddle for a dish-free breakfast.

Peel, chop, and measure out **ONIONS AND OTHER HARDY VEGGIES** like carrots, celery, anything that won't brown. Remaining steps can be written right onto the bag they're sealed in for an easy way to follow the recipe.

Measure out and mix **SPICES** into small baggies or containers and mark which recipe each is for. This saves you a binful of rattling spice jars to deal with. If you're particularly pinched for space—if you're backpacking, for example—you can even store bits of spices in a plastic straw snipped to size, with each end sealed shut with a candle or lighter flame.

Cut up bulky **FRUIT** such as melons and pineapples to save on space and to prevent a sticky mess at the site. Bring the slices or bite-sized pieces in a resealable container.

Do Ahead

Pancake mix kept in a resealable bag can have milk added at the site. Then, just snip off a corner and squeeze the batter right onto the griddle.

How to
SET UP CAMP

When you arrive, check out your site. Locate a good spot to set up the tent, one that's flat and not rocky. Check the ground for signs of rain runoff. You don't want to set up your tent in a spot that becomes a pool after a shower. Ideally your tent will be set up with some degree of privacy—facing a stand of trees or an open area away from other sites.

If nightfall is coming, **LOCATE YOUR LANTERN AND HEADLAMPS** right away so the darkness doesn't shut down the process. Everyone should have their own flashlight or headlamp, and kids can wear their headlamps like a necklace so they're handy when the time comes. Choose a spot for the car key and make sure all the adults know where it is.

Take the time to **GET YOUR COOKING AREA SET UP** well. Create an area for cooking, one for eating, another for washing (this is one reason an extra folding table comes in handy). A large plastic liquid laundry detergent container with a spigot, after being rinsed out thoroughly and filled with water, makes a simple handwashing station. Place it on a tree stump or rock and put a small bottle of biodegradable soap next to it, so people can easily wash up before eating or helping with meals.

DIVIDE AND CONQUER. While one team works on setting up the tent and blowing up sleeping pads, another can get the table area organized. Kids can learn a lot by pitching in however they can. If they're truly underfoot, task them with gathering kindling nearby. (Check at the ranger kiosk as you pull in—some campgrounds don't allow wood gathering.)

KEEP AN EYE ON YOUR FOOD. Wily raccoons, jays, and chipmunks (and, in some places, bears) look for any opportunity to grab a snack. Stay near the food and cooler until everything is put away.

Once you have things pretty well organized at the site, **EXPLORE THE CAMPGROUND** a bit. You can scope out the nearest bathroom and water faucet, locate any showers, find out if there's a ranger program, chat up other campers about their gear or any wildlife sightings. If you have kids along, be sure they know your site number and can lead the way back to your site.

Handy Tips

TIP: If your tent doesn't come with a built-in doormat (a number of Coleman tents do), a tatami mat unrolled outside the tent flap makes a nice front "porch," a place to leave shoes before stepping inside.

TIP: If rain is likely and your tent is at all down a slope, dig a small trench just uphill from your tent to channel any rain runoff away from it.

TIP: Coleman's stainless steel tablecloth clamps are handy for keeping the tablecloth from blowing away in the wind and fit most table thicknesses. In a pinch, a few stones gathered and rinsed will do the trick. Another pretty anchor is to put a row of tea lights into clean glass baby food jars down the middle of the table. These can be lit at mealtime for a simple and functional centerpiece.

Handy Tip

If you find you've under-packed for a cold night, there is a quick fix: Place some rocks at the edge of the fire for a few minutes (only a few!), wrap them in a shirt you don't mind messing up, and put them at the foot of your sleeping bag to ward off the chill. Another idea: Warm some water to nearly boiling and pour it into a Nalgene bottle for a modern-day bed warmer.

⋚ TIPS ON KEEPING THINGS ORGANIZED AND EFFICIENT ⋚

THINK ONE MEAL AHEAD

To minimize your cooking time, think of meals in pairs:

※ Before cleaning up after breakfast, go ahead and pack a portable lunch for the hike or the beach. That way you only have to clean up once.

※ Consider in the morning whether there are any meats or sauces that should be defrosted for dinner.

※ As you clean up after dinner, organize things for a quick cup of coffee and an easy breakfast in the morning.

KEEP YOUR TOOLS AT HAND

※ A wire clothes hanger threaded through a paper towel roll and hung over a branch comes in handy for quick cleanups.

※ A hanging shoe organizer works beautifully for keeping your silverware and other kitchen tools handy and organized. Strap it to a tree with a bungee or belt.

※ Run a line between two trees to easily hang up damp dish towels, clothes, and swimsuits.

※ Run a bungee cord or belt snugly around a tree trunk. Hung with S clips, it makes a nice hanging pot rack.

⋚ Handy Tips ⋚

TIP: Whenever possible, let one item do the job of two. A pot makes a perfectly fine salad bowl, and drinking wine out of a camping mug is better than fussing over a delicate wineglass. Thinking outside the box makes camping more of an adventure and minimizes the amount of packing and cleaning you have to do.

TIP: The recipes in this book rely heavily on a pair of cast-iron skillets and a Dutch oven. Yes, these are much heavier than the lightweight nesting pot sets sold specifically for camping. But they earn their weight by being ridiculously reliable, durable, and versatile. The Dutch oven is useful for soups, chilies, and boiling water. As its name suggests, it also works as a portable oven, allowing you to make all kinds of dishes you might think are off the list for camping—even cakes!

CRITTER CONTROL

Sure, sharing the great outdoors with the local animals is part of the point of camping, but cohabitating peacefully sometimes takes some strategizing. Here are tips on how to get along.

BEARS

When camping in bear country, special rules apply. If you're in an established campground, there will likely be metal bear boxes where you'll be required to keep your food, toiletries, sunscreen, and anything else that smells potentially tasty. Rangers sometimes levy hefty fines for leaving your food out—or even in your car—when you're not actively prepping a meal. Find out what the dimensions of the bear box are so you can make sure your coolers and food bins will fit.

✳ **TIP:** These metal boxes can get hot in the sun, which doesn't do your food any favors. Keep the temperature down by soaking a blanket in water and draping it over the bear box before you go off on your day's adventures.

SQUIRRELS, CHIPMUNKS, RACCOONS, AND JAYS

These little creatures are more nuisance than problem. Notoriously persistent, they'll leap, swoop, or scurry at any opportunity to grab a bite of your food. The solution is vigilance: stick near the table while you're prepping food, and put everything away when you're not. Plastic bins are more critter proof than grocery bags or cardboard boxes. Keep in mind that raccoons are remarkably good with their paws and can open a simple latch or a lid without a problem. You can discourage them by putting something heavy on the lids of any bins, jamming a thin branch through a hooking latch, and stashing stuff in the car (or bear box) before you wander off or go to sleep. Bring some steel wool to stuff into any big cracks or holes in the site's food box to make it more critter proof.

MOSQUITOES

ON YOUR SKIN: Repellents with DEET will last longest. Natural repellents will need to be reapplied often—probably every hour.

ON YOUR CLOTHES: Spraying permethrin deters mosquitoes and ticks. It works only on your clothes, not on your skin.

AT THE SITE: On a calm evening, citronella candles help keep mosquitoes at bay. If you have extra sage in your fridge or garden, tie it into bundles with string and toss the bundles in the fire to repel mosquitoes in a nontoxic, good-smelling way. A mosquito coil is another slow-burning option that doesn't blow out as easily as a candle. Both of these help most in calm conditions, when the aroma stays close. Some like to put a portable netted tent around their table area. But keep in mind, cooking at a site usually involves a lot of trips to the car or the bear box to grab more ingredients and tools, so you'll be opening the net often.

WASPS AND YELLOW JACKETS

When stinging pests swarm, it can really take the fun out of cooking and eating outdoors. An ounce of prevention will help. Choose a spot that's not adjacent to the campground's trash cans or dumpster if possible, and clean up any spills quickly. Some people erect a mesh net around their picnic table so they can prep and eat in peace. Others swear by simple repellents like hanging dryer sheets around the campsite or leaving sliced cucumber around. There's also the opposite approach—putting a piece of meat or something sweet a few yards from your site to tempt them away.

You can make an easy DIY trap by cutting the top third off a 2-liter plastic soda bottle, putting a half inch of sugary beverage and a couple drops of dish soap into the bottom, and then placing the top upside down on the bottom. Wasps and yellow jackets will be drawn to the liquid and will be unable to get back out.

BRIDGER–TETON NATIONAL FOREST, WYOMING

How to
TEND THE FIRE

Most of the recipes in this book can be made on a campfire or on a camping stove, but let's face it: You've got to have a campfire. The fire is the campsite's hearth, and everyone will gather around to chat and warm up and watch the flames dance.

START WITH A GOOD PILE OF FUEL

Check with the campground for any restrictions on wood burning. Some spots allow you to burn only wood from on-site (to avoid spreading tree diseases); others forbid any wood gathering in the campground—all wood must be bought from the host or brought in.

Wherever you source your wood, aim for a mix of sizes, from **TINDER** (dry grass, newspaper, pine needles) and **KINDLING** (small, thin, dry sticks) to get the fire going, up to large, dense **LOGS** that will keep the fire going for hours. It can be handy to bring a small hatchet in case you need to break up bigger pieces to get the sizes you need. Avoid wood that isn't thoroughly dried out if you can—it can be very smoky, chasing people away from the fire.

FIRE STARTERS TO GET YOUR BLAZE GOING

You can easily buy fuel-soaked starters, but it's also quite simple to prep effective starters at home that work beautifully and are less toxic.

One **CLASSIC BOY SCOUT TRICK** is to stuff each of the dozen spots in a cardboard egg carton with dryer lint. Melt down some old candle wax (you can put it into a saved food can and half-submerge it in boiling water). Pour the melted wax over each ball of lint. After the wax cools and hardens, you can snip it into individual mini-starters or leave it as is for one heckuva bonfire booster. A simpler version of this idea is simply to load up an egg carton with a dozen pieces of charcoal and light the cardboard.

Other **QUICK BOOSTS FOR A STRUGGLING FIRE:** birthday candles (so much the better if you have a trick one you can't blow out), a squirt of hand sanitizer, a cotton ball soaked in petroleum jelly, alcohol pads from your first aid kit, cotton pads dipped in wax, or even a fluffed-up tampon. Yes, seriously.

Handy Tip

TIP: The strike side of a matchbox nearly always wears out before the matches run out, which can lead to much frustration and cursing in front of the kids. An easy fix is to find a small plastic container (maybe a child's snack container) and attach a piece of sandpaper to one side. This will work better and last longer than a store-bought box of matches.

BUILD A GOOD COOKING FIRE

TO MAKE A FIRE WORK WELL FOR COOKING, AS WELL AS FOR ENTERTAINMENT, THERE ARE A FEW TIPS TO KEEP IN MIND:

START IT EARLY Outsmart camp cooking's major pitfall—not starting the fire early enough. Figure on starting the fire at least an hour before you want to start cooking. Coals cook so much more effectively than flames.

BEGIN WITH A TIPI Around a small pile of tinder, lean some small sticks against each other to form a tipi and light the pile of tinder. Blow gently at the bottom of it until the flames get going.

CONTROL FLARE-UPS It helps to leave a section of the fire ring pretty clear of coals. This way, if a piece of food flares up (probably from dripping grease onto the fire), you can move the food away from the heat for a bit to regain control of the situation. This works better than squirting water at a flare up, which mostly serves only to get ashes all over your food. This cool zone in the fire is also helpful in case one piece of food cooks more quickly than another—it gives you more control over the timing.

GROW IT SLOWLY It's easy to extinguish a just-started fire with enthusiasm. Don't plop a log onto your burning tipi or you'll be starting from scratch. For awhile, just lean slightly larger sticks against each other to make a bigger and bigger tipi around your fire. Once it's going strong, you can build a log cabin of logs around it or simply lay a couple of small logs against each other, always keeping some space underneath for oxygen to circulate.

WAIT FOR THE GLOW
The best fire for cooking has passed the high flames stage and has become more of a bed of coals. This will make for consistent heat and will give you a large area to cook over (or in). Keep a log burning off to the side in case your coals start fading.

HEAT THE GRILL
If you use the metal grill that's attached to the fire ring, it may need a wipe-down with an oily paper towel to prevent food from sticking to it. It definitely needs to be nice and hot before you put any food on it.

PUT IT OUT COMPLETELY Don't mess around with this task—warm coals can reignite when you've gone to bed or wandered off. The last person to bed is responsible for pouring water onto the coals, stirring them around, and pouring some more, until there is no warmth or glow at all.

FIRE SAFETY TIP

If you're camping in the backcountry, be sure to check for any fire restrictions before heading out. In general, fires should only be built where there is already a fire ring. Depending on conditions, sometimes fires are limited to charcoal or forbidden altogether. In this case, you'll want to bump up how many scarves and mittens you bring.

⁝ KEEP THE KIDS BUSY WHILE YOU COOK ⁝

If you're camping with a hungry crew of kids, it can be helpful for you—and a fun surprise for them—to prep a few simple activities they can tackle while dinner is being prepared.

If gathering wood is allowed, put the kids in charge of tracking down enough kindling to **REPLENISH THE WOOD PILE.**

Get them exploring the campground with a simple scavenger hunt craft. Ring some duct tape around their wrists with the sticky side out, then send them off to find leaves, flowers, and small pebbles or shells to stick onto their **"CAMPING BRACELET."**

For a buck or two, you can buy each kid a simple balsa-wood kit to **PUT TOGETHER A GLIDER.** Between assembling these and launching them from on top of every stump around, this should keep them busy for a while.

SHUCKING CORN is an easy job for kids—and infinitely more fun when you're allowed to toss leaves and silks right into the fire.

Kids who have learned some knife skills may welcome the chance to **USE A POCKETKNIFE** for real on simple slicing and dicing tasks that will keep them busy and help with meal prep.

Have the kids collaborate on **DRAWING A MAP** of the campsite and the surrounding area. They can hide some found treasures like acorns or river rocks and mark the spot with an X.

Tips for CLEANING UP

This is no one's favorite topic, but a few tips will make cleanup relatively painless.

TIPS FOR KEEPING THE CAMPSITE TIDY

✳ **CREATE A FRONT PORCH. If your tent** doesn't have one already built in, put a tatami mat, flattened cardboard box, or folded tarp outside your tent's entrance. This way you won't track dirt inside, and you'll have a clean place to put on your shoes.

✳ **KEEP A TRASH BAG HUNG IN A HANDY SPOT.** There will often be a nail sticking out of the food box you can hang it from, or you can use a small branch of a tree. (Note: Depending on bear regulations, you may need to put your trash into the bear box.)

✳ **BRING BABY WIPES. They work wonders** for a quick wipe-down of the table, on-the-go handwashing, or cleaning up any gear that gets sticky or dirty.

✳ **PUT EVERYTHING AWAY AT NIGHT.** Nocturnal creatures will have a heyday with anything left loose. Make sure food and cooking supplies go back into bins and jackets and shoes are brought back into tents.

HOW TO WASH DISHES AT A CAMPSITE

RELAX YOUR STANDARDS. It's tricky to get dishes as clean as they would be at home. Let it go and let pretty good be good enough.

MINIMIZE THE PILE OF DISHES. Let your coffee mug do double duty as your oatmeal bowl, say, and you'll have fewer dishes to wash up after breakfast.

WARM SOME WATER. Washing dishes in cold water is no fun. Before you sit down to eat, fill your biggest pot with water and put it on to heat. If you have a good fire going, put it over the fire—warming water on a camping stove burns up a lot of fuel. By the time you finish eating, you'll have nice warm water to work with.

START WITH A QUICK WIPE. Go over greasy pans/plates with paper towels before washing, so the water doesn't get too dirty, too fast.

GO EASY ON THE SOAP. Put just a couple of drops of biodegradable soap into the pot of water you've heated. Wash dishes in this, leaving the dirtiest ones for last.

RINSE. If you have another container of warm or hot water for this, great. Otherwise, deputize someone to take the washed but soapy dishes in piles to the cold water tap to give them a quick rinse and bring them back.

DRY BEFORE PUTTING AWAY. Deputize someone else to dry off the rinsed dishes before putting them back in their bin.

A WORD ON YOUR CAST-IRON SKILLETS AND DUTCH OVEN

If your cast-iron pans retain their seasoning, they'll be relatively nonstick and easy to clean. Here's how to keep them primed and ready for the next meal.

DON'T DELAY. The best time to clean a cast-iron pan is while it's still warm.

DO A PREWIPE. If there's food left in the pan, wipe it out with a paper towel. A bit of salt or even dirt poured into the pan makes an effective natural abrasive for attacking any grease or stubborn crust.

SKIP THE SOAP. Wash your pan with just hot water and a cloth or plastic scrubber. Soap can erode the seasoning on the pan.

DRY THOROUGHLY. Once the pan is clean, put it over heat until it's fully dry. Wipe it out with a paper towel doused with vegetable oil and put it away for next time.

Handy Tips

TIP: Use a spare folding table or a nearby picnic table to set up a space for dish washing. You can have an assembly line of a pot of soapy water, a pot of fresh warm water for rinsing, and a couple of dish towels for drying. Coleman has a folding double wash basin that can be a useful tool to have on site.

TIP: If you've been grilling, try to scrape any bits of food off the grill while it's still hot. This is much easier and more effective than trying to do it once the grill has cooled.

Tips for

PACKING UP

Follow these tips for organizing your gear for the trip home—and for keeping it in order for your next outdoor adventure.

FIRST, CHOOSE YOUR PACKING STRATEGY

STRATEGY 1:
DO IT RIGHT, DO IT ONCE

Many campers believe in taking the time before driving home to dry out, wipe down, and pack up the gear so that it can go straight into storage from the car. If you go this route, it will take some time at the campsite to clean up anything (everything!) that has gotten dirty. It helps to have a hand broom for dusting off dirt and disposable wipes or a damp rag for cleaning up gear. Some chores, like cleaning out the cooler, will need to wait till you get home.

STRATEGY 2:
DO THE REAL WORK AT HOME

The second strategy is to simply get your gear into the car however you can, the idea being that it will be easier to dry out tarps when you can stretch them out in your yard and easier to clean dishes when you have your dishwasher (or at least hot running water) at the ready. If you have enough room in your car, you can loosely roll up sleeping bags and pads and air them out at home. Dishes from the last breakfast can simply be tossed into a trash bag and washed later. Your departure will be quicker, though you'll need to devote some time when you get home to putting things in order.

HOW TO GET THE KIDS INVOLVED

Small cleanup tasks will begin teaching children how to become good campers and will also keep them busy while you wrestle the camping chairs back into their bags. Kids love to deflate the **SLEEPING PADS.** (They're less good at rolling them up tightly and wiggling them into their stuff sacks.) Pulling the **POLES OUT OF THE TENT** and collapsing it flat is also a favorite.

Kids are very eager to pour water on the **FIRE** and stir the ash around to be certain there are no coals, and no warmth at all.

When the campsite is getting close to being packed up, challenge the kids to see who can pick up the most little **BITS OF TRASH.** Make it a contest. Many small hands make light work.

The kids can also be in charge of carrying the **TRASH BAG TO THE DUMPSTER** (or getting it to the car if there isn't one). Point out that disposing of the trash is important not only because it's considerate of the next campers, but because it's essential for the animals' safety. Kids should learn the camper's credo that you always leave your site at least as clean as you found it.

BACK AT HOME
STEPS YOU'LL THANK YOURSELF FOR THE NEXT TIME:

TURN UNPACKING INTO PREPACKING

Frequent campers develop a knack for prepacking for their next trip as they pack away the gear from the current one. If you have a packing checklist, print out a copy and check off items as you put them into the bins, taping the checklist to the bin when you're done, so the next time you get the gear out you know for sure what's already packed and ready.

DON'T STORE SLEEPING BAGS AND PADS IN THEIR STUFF SACKS

They last longer, stay fluffier, and avoid getting mildewy if you air them thoroughly, and then hang them up or at least lay them flat.

SCRUB OUT THE COOLER

See page 12 for tips on cleaning your cooler, and then leave it to dry completely in the sun before shutting the lid and packing it away.

WIPE DOWN YOUR CAMPING STOVE WITH WARM WATER AND A BIT OF DISH SOAP

If you've had a messy boil over, you can also disassemble the stove to clean the parts individually in the sink. Instructions should be in the manual. You'll want to pack your stove away clean so it doesn't entice any insects or other pests while in storage.

SIUSLAW NATIONAL
FOREST, OREGON

Chapter One

BREAKFAST

GOOD MORNING CHEDDAR DROP BISCUITS AND SAUSAGE GRAVY

HANDS-ON: 20 MINUTES | **TOTAL:** 35 MINUTES | SERVES 6

Drop biscuits are the easiest biscuits to make since there's no rolling or cutting required, an ideal and filling camping breakfast. The tasty sage-enhanced gravy comes together easily while the biscuits cook.

¼ cup unsalted butter, melted, divided
2 cups all-purpose baking mix (such as Bisquick)
2 ounces sharp Cheddar cheese, shredded (about ½ cup)
4 ¼ cups whole milk, divided
1 pound pork breakfast sausage
⅓ cup (about 1½ ounces) all-purpose flour
½ teaspoon kosher salt
½ teaspoon black pepper
⅛ teaspoon dried sage

1. Heat a camping stove to medium (about 350° to 450°F), or fit a grilling grate over the direct heat of glowing embers. Cut 6 (18-inch) squares of aluminum foil; crumple each foil square into a 1½- to 2-inch ball. Arrange foil balls on the bottom of a 4½- to 5-quart cast-iron Dutch oven. Cover with the lid, and preheat on the camping stove or on a grilling grate directly over heat source 10 minutes.

2. Grease a 9-inch round cake pan with 1 tablespoon of the melted butter. Combine the baking mix, cheese, ¾ cup of the milk, and 2 tablespoons of the melted butter in a medium bowl, stirring just until combined. Drop the dough by heaping tablespoonfuls into the greased cake pan. Place the pan on top of the foil balls in the preheated Dutch oven; cover with the lid. Bake until the biscuits are browned on bottom and done, 30 to 35 minutes.

3. Meanwhile, place a 12-inch cast-iron skillet over medium on a camping stove or on a grilling grate directly over the heat source. Add the sausage, and cook, stirring until the sausage crumbles and is no longer pink, 6 to 8 minutes. Stir in the remaining 1 tablespoon melted butter. Sprinkle the flour over the mixture; stir to combine, and cook 1 minute. Slowly stir in the remaining 3½ cups milk until combined. Cook, stirring often, until the mixture begins to thicken, 8 to 10 minutes. Stir in the salt, pepper, and sage. Serve the gravy over the biscuits.

CANADIAN BACON, TOMATO, AND EGG CAMPFIRE STACKS

HANDS-ON: 20 MINUTES | **TOTAL:** 20 MINUTES | SERVES 4

Serve this hearty breakfast sandwich before a day of hiking. The lemony mayonnaise complements the smoky bacon, elevating this sandwich to the highest peak.

4 English muffins, split and lightly buttered on cut sides
3 tablespoons unsalted butter, divided
8 Canadian bacon slices
6 large eggs
½ teaspoon kosher salt
¼ teaspoon black pepper
¼ cup mayonnaise
1 tablespoon fresh lemon juice
¼ teaspoon smoked paprika
4 ripe tomato slices (from 1 medium tomato)

1. Heat a camping stove to medium-high (about 375° to 400°F), or fit a grilling grate over the direct heat of glowing embers. Preheat a 10-inch cast-iron skillet on the camping stove or grilling grate 5 minutes. Place the muffin halves, buttered side down, in the skillet, and cook until lightly toasted, 3 to 4 minutes. Remove the muffins from the skillet, and set aside. Melt 1 tablespoon of the butter in the skillet; add the bacon slices, and cook until lightly browned, about 2 minutes per side. Remove the bacon slices from skillet, and set aside. Wipe the skillet clean.

2. Whisk together the eggs, salt, and pepper in a medium bowl until combined. Melt the remaining 2 tablespoons butter in the skillet; add the eggs, and cook, without stirring, until the eggs start to set on bottom. Continue cooking, stirring occasionally, until desired degree of doneness.

3. Stir together the mayonnaise, lemon juice, and smoked paprika. Place one bacon slice on the toasted side of each of four muffin halves; top evenly with cooked eggs. Top each with one tomato slice, another bacon slice, and a dollop of lemon mayonnaise. Cover with the remaining muffin halves, and serve immediately.

THINK LIKE A SCOUT

To save space in your cooler, you can crack and gently mix the eggs at home, and then use a funnel to pour them into a water bottle or other leakproof container. They'll store safely for a couple of days once out of their shells. When you're ready to cook, just give them a gentle shake and pour them into the skillet. If you prefer to bring whole eggs, use a Coleman® egg container to safely store them in your cooler. It's also handy for transporting hard-boiled eggs.

KITCHEN SINK FRITTATA

HANDS-ON: 15 MINUTES | **TOTAL:** 50 MINUTES | SERVES 6

Rather than taking leftovers home and unpacking them into your fridge, serve this breakfast the last morning and toss in any leftover steak, sausage, bratwurst, peppers, onions, veggies, etc. (get creative!) for a leftovers adventure.

1 tablespoon olive oil

12 ounces smoked sausage, sliced

½ cup vertically sliced red or sweet onion (about 1½ ounces)

½ cup chopped tomato (about 2½ ounces)

2 cups coarsely chopped spinach, Swiss chard, or kale
    (about 3 ounces)

8 large eggs, lightly beaten

1 cup heavy cream

4 ounces sharp white Cheddar cheese, shredded (about 1 cup)

½ teaspoon kosher salt

¼ teaspoon black pepper

2 ounces feta cheese, crumbled (about ½ cup)

1. Heat a camping stove to medium (about 350° to 375°F). Preheat a 10-inch cast-iron skillet with a lid on the camping stove for 5 minutes. Heat the oil in the skillet; add the sausage, and cook, stirring occasionally, until lightly browned, about 5 minutes. Drain the drippings from the sausage, reserving about 1 tablespoon in the skillet. Add the onions and tomatoes to the skillet, and cook, stirring often, until the onions soften and the tomatoes start to blister, about 4 minutes. Add the spinach, and cook, stirring until wilted, about 1 minute.

2. Whisk together the eggs, cream, white Cheddar, salt, and pepper in a large bowl. Pour the egg mixture over the sausage mixture in the skillet, and cook until the eggs just start to set up on the bottom and outside edges of the skillet. Gently draw the eggs from the edges to the center of the skillet, allowing most of the mixture to remain soft set. Reduce the camping stove heat to very low (about 250° to 275°F). Sprinkle the feta cheese over the top of the mixture in the skillet, and cook until the eggs are set, 30 to 35 minutes, covering with the lid halfway through cooking time. (Do not let the eggs become dry or burned on bottom.) Remove the skillet from the heat, and let the frittata stand 5 minutes. Cut into six wedges, and serve immediately.

SOUTHWEST CHILAQUILES SKILLET BREAKFAST

HANDS-ON: 15 MINUTES | **TOTAL:** 28 MINUTES | SERVES 6

Mexican chorizo easily crumbles, unlike its Spanish counterpart, which is dried, cured, and similar to salami.

THINK LIKE A SCOUT

Paper cartons of milk, half-and-half, and cream have a way of leaking in the cooler, especially when they're submerged in water from the melting ice. Keep things tidier by buying your dairy in plastic or glass leakproof containers for the trip.

10 ounces fresh Mexican chorizo, casing removed
1 medium-sized red bell pepper, diced
½ cup diced poblano chile (from 1 small chile)
½ cup vertically sliced red onion (from 1 small onion)
½ teaspoon kosher salt
¼ teaspoon black pepper
12 corn tortillas, coarsely chopped
8 large eggs, lightly beaten
4 ounces Monterey Jack cheese, shredded (about 1 cup)
2 ounces pepper Jack cheese, shredded (about ½ cup)
⅓ cup whole milk
½ cup chopped fresh cilantro
Hot sauce
Sour cream

1. Heat a camping stove to medium-high (about 375° to 400°F). Preheat a 10- x 3-inch cast-iron fryer with a lid on the camping stove for 5 minutes. Add the chorizo, and cook, stirring to crumble, until cooked through, 6 to 8 minutes. Using a slotted spoon, remove the chorizo to drain on a plate lined with paper towels. Add the bell pepper, poblano, onions, salt, and pepper to the fryer, and cook, stirring often, until the vegetables are softened and lightly browned, 4 to 6 minutes. Stir in the chopped tortillas.

2. Stir together the eggs, cheeses, and milk in a medium bowl. Return the chorizo to the fryer, and stir to combine with the tortilla mixture. Pour the egg mixture over the top, and cook until the eggs just start to set on the bottom and outside edges of the fryer. Gently draw the eggs from the outside edges to the center, repeating the process until the mixture is very loosely set. Reduce the camping stove heat to low (about 275° to 300°F). Cover the fryer, and cook until the eggs are set and the mixture is cooked through, 8 to 10 minutes. Sprinkle with the cilantro, and serve with the hot sauce and sour cream on the side.

GRILLED VEGETABLE AND BLACK BEAN BREAKFAST BURRITOS

HANDS-ON: 20 MINUTES | **TOTAL:** 25 MINUTES | SERVES 4

The mashed bean mixture acts as a barrier between the tortilla and the vegetable and egg mixtures, so the burritos stay crisp.

1 (15-ounce) can seasoned black beans, undrained
1 tablespoon olive oil
1 small zucchini, diced
1 small yellow squash, diced
1 cup vertically sliced sweet onion (about 1 small onion)
1 cup seeded and thinly sliced poblano chile (about 1 small chile)
1 teaspoon ground cumin
¾ teaspoon kosher salt, divided
½ teaspoon black pepper, divided
6 large eggs, lightly beaten
¼ cup chopped fresh cilantro
8 ounces Monterey Jack cheese, shredded (about 2 cups), divided
1 tablespoon salted butter
4 burrito-sized flour tortillas
1 cup salsa, warmed
2 tablespoons hot sauce
½ cup sour cream

1. Heat a camping stove to medium-high (about 375° to 400°F), or fit a grilling grate over the direct heat of glowing embers. Place the beans in a medium saucepan on the camping stove or grilling grate, and cook, stirring and lightly mashing, until heated through, about 5 minutes. Remove from the heat, and cover to keep warm.

2. Preheat a 10-inch cast-iron skillet on the camping stove or the grilling grate for 5 minutes; add the oil. Add the zucchini and squash, and cook until slightly softened, 2 to 3 minutes. Add the onions, poblano, cumin, ½ teaspoon of the salt, and ¼ teaspoon of the pepper; cook, stirring often, until the vegetables are softened and lightly browned, about 6 minutes. Remove the mixture from the skillet, and keep warm. Wipe the skillet clean.

3. Stir together the eggs, cilantro, ½ cup of the cheese, and the remaining ¼ teaspoon each of the salt and pepper. Melt the butter in the skillet on the camping stove or grilling grate; add the egg mixture, and cook just until the eggs start to set on the bottom. Gently stir the mixture, cooking just until the eggs are soft scrambled or until desired degree of doneness. Remove the skillet from the heat.

4. Arrange the tortillas on a grilling grate directly over the heat source, and cook until lightly charred, about 30 seconds per side.

5. Spread about ⅓ cup mashed black beans over each tortilla, leaving
a 1-inch border. Spoon about ¾ cup vegetables in the center; sprinkle with
about ⅓ cup shredded cheese, and top with about ½ cup scrambled egg
mixture. Fold opposite sides of the tortilla over the filling, and roll up.
Stir together the salsa and hot sauce. Top each burrito evenly with sour
cream and the warmed salsa mixture. Serve immediately.

CRESTED BUTTE, COLORADO

RAINBOW TROUT HASH AND EGGS

HANDS-ON: 25 MINUTES | **TOTAL:** 30 MINUTES | SERVES 4

Use leftover grilled trout freshly caught or packaged smoked trout that you "caught" at the supermarket.

1 small sweet potato (about 8 ounces), peeled and diced
2 red potatoes (about 8 ounces), unpeeled and diced
4 thick-cut bacon slices, cut into ½-inch pieces
1 medium-sized yellow bell pepper (about 8 ounces), diced
1 cup diced red onion (about 1 small onion)
½ teaspoon kosher salt
¼ teaspoon black pepper
⅛ teaspoon red pepper flakes
8 ounces cooked or smoked trout fillets, cut into 1½-inch pieces
1½ tablespoons fresh lemon juice
2 tablespoons salted butter
4 large eggs
Hot sauce (optional)

1. Heat a camping stove to medium-high (about 375° to 400°F), or fit a grilling grate over the direct heat of glowing embers. Bring a medium saucepan of salted water to a boil on camping stove or grilling grate. Add the sweet potatoes, and cook 2 minutes. Add red potatoes, and cook until potatoes are almost tender, 4 to 5 minutes. Drain well; spread potatoes in a single layer on a baking sheet, and let dry.

2. Preheat a 10-inch cast-iron skillet on the camping stove or grilling grate 5 minutes. Add bacon pieces, and cook, stirring often, until crispy, about 6 minutes. Remove bacon, and drain on a large plate lined with paper towels, reserving the drippings in the skillet. Add the bell pepper, onions, salt, black pepper, and red pepper to hot drippings in skillet, and cook, stirring often, until vegetables are just starting to soften, about 4 minutes. Using a slotted spoon, remove vegetable mixture to drain on paper towels with bacon.

3. Spread the potatoes in a single layer in skillet, and cook, undisturbed, until golden brown on bottom, about 4 minutes. Turn potatoes, and cook 3 minutes. Return vegetable mixture and bacon to skillet; add trout pieces, and cook, stirring gently so trout pieces stay intact, until warmed through, 1 to 2 minutes. Sprinkle lemon juice over trout mixture in skillet, and stir gently. Remove trout mixture from skillet, and keep warm. Wipe skillet clean.

4. Melt the butter in skillet. Crack the eggs, one at a time, into skillet, and cook until desired degree of doneness. Divide trout mixture evenly among four serving plates; top each with an egg, and serve immediately. Serve with hot sauce on the side, if desired.

GETTING
GEARED UP

If you plan to try your luck with fishing, check with the campground to see if they have a cleaning station—some that are near prime fishing spots do. If not, add to your packing list a fillet knife, scaling tool, and a bucket or some other container for discarding the unwanted parts. Your camping buddies will appreciate your setting up a separate area to handle this task.

CAMP SHAKSHUKA AND FRENCH BREAD

HANDS-ON: 20 MINUTES | **TOTAL:** 40 MINUTES | SERVES 4

This North African dish features eggs poached in a spicy and bright tomato ragout. Served over charred French bread, this meal will leave you warm and satisfied on the coldest days.

12 ounces Italian pork sausage, casing removed
1 cup vertically sliced sweet onion (about 1 small onion)
½ cup vertically sliced red onion (from 1 small onion)
½ cup chopped pimiento-stuffed olives
2 tablespoons vegetable oil
4 garlic cloves, chopped
1 (28-ounce) can San Marzano tomatoes, undrained
    and lightly chopped
1 tablespoon dried oregano
½ teaspoon smoked paprika
¼ teaspoon kosher salt
¼ teaspoon black pepper
4 large eggs
1 (6-ounce) baguette, cut into 4 (½-inch-thick) slices
2 tablespoons olive oil
1 ounce Parmesan cheese, shaved (about ½ cup)

1. Heat a camping stove to medium-high (about 375° to 400°F), or fit a grilling grate over the direct heat of glowing embers. Preheat a 12-inch cast-iron skillet with a lid on the camping stove or grilling grate for 5 minutes. Add the sausage, and cook, stirring to crumble, until cooked through and lightly browned, about 8 minutes. Remove the sausage from the skillet, and drain on a large plate lined with paper towels.

2. Add the onions, olives, vegetable oil, and garlic to the skillet; cook, stirring occasionally, until the onions are softened and lightly browned, about 6 minutes. Reduce the heat to medium (about 350° to 375°F). Stir in the tomatoes, oregano, paprika, salt, pepper, and sausage, and simmer, stirring occasionally, until slightly thickened, about 20 minutes. Using the back of a spoon, form 4 indentations in the meat sauce. Crack one egg into each indentation; cover the skillet with the lid, and cook until the whites are set but the yolks are still runny, 6 to 8 minutes.

3. Brush both sides of the bread slices with the olive oil, and place on the grilling grate directly over the heat source. Grill until lightly charred and crispy, about 2 minutes per side. Place one bread slice on each of four plates; spoon the meat sauce evenly over the bread. Top each with one egg, and sprinkle with Parmesan.

STRAWBERRIES AND CREAM OF WHEAT

HANDS-ON: 10 MINUTES | **TOTAL:** 15 MINUTES | SERVES 6

Give your Cream of Wheat a boost with sweet summer berries and tart crème fraîche. Make this the first morning of your trip, since fragile strawberries don't last long in the cooler, or substitute any seasonal berry for the strawberries.

4 cups whole milk

¾ cup uncooked Cream of Wheat cereal

¼ cup honey

1 cup chopped plus 1½ cups quartered fresh strawberries
   (about 1 quart), divided

1 teaspoon vanilla extract

1 tablespoon fresh lemon juice

6 tablespoons crème fraîche

2 tablespoons granulated sugar

1. Heat a camping stove to medium-high (about 375° to 400°F), or fit a grilling grate over the direct heat of glowing embers. Bring the milk to a boil in a large saucepan on the camping stove or grilling grate, stirring occasionally. Add the Cream of Wheat and honey, and cook, stirring constantly, until thickened, 3 to 5 minutes. Stir in the chopped strawberries and vanilla. Remove from the heat.

2. Toss together the quartered strawberries and lemon juice. Spoon the prepared cereal mixture into each of six bowls; top evenly with the quartered strawberries, crème fraîche, and sugar. Serve immediately.

HOW TO
MAKE COFFEE AT **CAMP**

FIRST THINGS FIRST

How do you get a good cup of coffee when your coffeemaker is back home on your kitchen counter? Fortunately, there are several simple ways to brew on the go.

CONE DIP
These mug-top cones come in ceramic and plastic models, some of which even fold flat for backpackers.

FRENCH PRESS
Outdoors stores sell versions with neoprene on the outside to hold in warmth and make them more durable than bare glass.

EUROPEAN-STYLE STOVETOP POT
The water goes into the bottom half, the grounds are packed in between, and coffee bubbles up on top. Just as good as you remember it from your trip to Italy.

PERCOLATOR
These colorful speckled enamel pots with old-school charm show coffee bubbling up in the clear knob on top. When the color looks dark enough, you know it's ready.

CREAMY TOASTED OATS IN A SKILLET

HANDS-ON: 10 MINUTES | **TOTAL:** 20 MINUTES | SERVES 4

Can you say power breakfast?! This bowl of yumminess is packed with protein and the good kind of carbs to get you ready for a day on the trail. The nuttiness from browning the butter is a delicious pairing for the roasty almond butter.

2 ounces (¼ cup) salted butter
2 cups uncooked regular rolled oats
3½ cups hot water
¼ teaspoon kosher salt
¼ cup almond butter
1 teaspoon ground cinnamon
1 teaspoon vanilla extract
½ cup sweetened dried cranberries
¼ cup roasted, salted pistachios, chopped
1 large Fuji apple, diced (about 1 cup)
Pure maple syrup (optional)

1. Heat a camping stove to medium-high (about 375° to 400°F), or fit a grilling grate over the direct heat of glowing embers. Place the butter in a 10-inch cast-iron skillet on the camping stove or grilling grate directly over the heat source, and cook, stirring occasionally, until the butter melts and begins to smell nutty, about 4 minutes. Add the oats to the skillet, and cook, stirring constantly, until the oats are toasted and fragrant, about 3 minutes.

2. Add 3½ cups hot water and salt to the skillet; stir until blended. Cook, stirring often, until the oats are tender and creamy, about 10 minutes. Stir in the almond butter, cinnamon, and vanilla. (If the oatmeal is not creamy enough for you, stir in more hot water, 1 tablespoon at a time, until desired consistency is reached.)

3. Spoon the oatmeal into each of four bowls; top with the cranberries, pistachios, diced apple, and, if desired, maple syrup.

DUTCH OVEN PEACH-OATMEAL BROWN BETTY

HANDS-ON: 12 MINUTES | **TOTAL:** 3 HOURS, 30 MINUTES | SERVES 6

This is a hearty oat-packed breakfast that could also double as a dessert with a dollop of whipped cream. Caramelizing the peaches before adding the oat mixture prevents the oatmeal from burning.

1 cup whole milk
½ cup packed light brown sugar
2 tablespoons fresh lemon juice (from 1 lemon)
2 teaspoons baking powder
½ teaspoon ground cinnamon
¼ teaspoon table salt
2 large eggs
2⅓ cups uncooked quick-cooking rolled oats
2 ounces (¼ cup) salted butter, melted, divided
1 (16-ounce) bag frozen peach slices, thawed and drained
½ cup granola

1. Whisk together the milk, brown sugar, lemon juice, baking powder, cinnamon, salt, and eggs in a large bowl. Stir in the oats and 2 tablespoons of the melted butter. Pour the mixture into a large ziplock plastic freezer bag; seal bag, and chill in a cooler or refrigerator at least 3 hours or overnight. (This is an excellent dish to make before leaving for your trip. Prepare step 1, and then proceed with step 2 when ready to cook.)

2. Heat a camping stove to medium-low (about 300° to 325°F), or fit a grilling grate over the direct heat of glowing embers. Grease a 4-quart cast-iron Dutch oven with a lid with the remaining 2 tablespoons butter, and add the peaches. Pour the oat mixture over the peaches; cover with the lid, and place on the camping stove or grilling grate. Cook until the oatmeal is puffed and cooked, 15 to 20 minutes. Sprinkle the granola over the top before serving.

BLUEBERRY-ALMOND PANCAKES

HANDS-ON: 15 MINUTES | **TOTAL:** 15 MINUTES | SERVES 4

If you prefer, substitute nutmeg and coriander with other warm spices, like cinnamon.

2 cups all-purpose baking mix (such as Bisquick)
½ cup dried blueberries, chopped
¼ teaspoon ground coriander
⅛ teaspoon ground nutmeg
1 tablespoon grated orange zest (from 1 orange), divided
1 cup whole milk
2 large eggs, lightly beaten
1 cup pure maple syrup
1 cup fresh blueberries
2 tablespoons salted butter
½ cup toasted sliced almonds

1. Heat a camping stove to medium-high (about 375° to 400°F), or fit a grilling grate over the direct heat of glowing embers.

2. Preheat a cast-iron griddle on the camping stove or grilling grate 8 minutes. Stir together the baking mix, chopped dried blueberries, coriander, nutmeg, and ½ tablespoon of the orange zest in a large bowl. Stir together the milk and eggs; add to the dry ingredients, and stir until combined.

3. Lightly grease the hot griddle. Pour about ¼ cup batter for each pancake onto the griddle, and cook until small bubbles appear on the surface. Turn and cook until cooked through, 1 to 2 minutes.

4. Stir together the syrup, fresh blueberries, butter, and remaining ½ tablespoon orange zest in a saucepan on the camping stove or grilling grate, and cook until the berries just begin to burst, about 6 minutes. Serve the pancakes with the warm syrup mixture and a sprinkle of toasted almonds.

THINK *Like* A SCOUT

To save on dishes, you can mix the pancake batter in a ziplock plastic bag. Just put in all the ingredients, zip it closed, and squeeze and slosh the bag with your hands. Then, cut one corner off, and you can use the bag like a frosting bag, squeezing dollops of batter onto the hot griddle, nice and tidy.

MONO COUNTY,
CALIFORNIA

LEMON-BLACKBERRY-RICOTTA WAFFLES WITH WHIPPED CREAM

HANDS-ON: 15 MINUTES | **TOTAL:** 25 MINUTES | SERVES 5

If desired, you can make the blackberry compote ahead and reheat it on the stove. If blackberries aren't in season, substitute any other berry that you like.

2 cups all-purpose baking mix (such as Bisquick)

1⅓ cups whole milk

½ cup ricotta cheese

2 tablespoons vegetable oil

1 large egg

2 tablespoons grated lemon zest (from 3 lemons), divided

2 pints fresh blackberries

1 cup pure maple syrup

2 ounces (¼ cup) salted butter, cut into pats

Refrigerated instant whipped cream (such as Reddi-wip; optional)

1. Heat a camping stove to medium-high (about 375° to 400°F), or fit a grilling grate over the direct heat of glowing embers. Whisk together the baking mix, milk, ricotta, oil, egg, and 1 tablespoon of the lemon zest in a large bowl.

2. Spoon about ⅓ cup batter into each side of a lightly greased waffle iron; close the lid, and lock. Place on the camping stove or grilling grate directly over the heat source, and cook until the waffles are crispy on the edges and cooked through, 4 to 5 minutes. Wrap the cooked waffles in aluminum foil to keep warm. Repeat the process with the remaining batter. Reduce the camping stove heat to medium (about 350° to 375°F).

3. Place the blackberries, maple syrup, and remaining 1 tablespoon lemon zest in a small saucepan, and cook, smashing the blackberries with the back of a spoon to break up, until warm, 6 to 8 minutes. Top each waffle with a pat of butter. Spoon the warm blackberry syrup over the waffles, and, if desired, dollop with whipped cream.

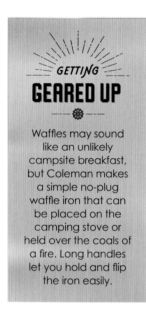

ELVIS GOES CAMPING

HANDS-ON: 20 MINUTES | **TOTAL:** 20 MINUTES | SERVES 5

Ripe bananas, crunchy peanut butter, and spiced, fluffy pancakes will power you through any vigorous day hike. Mix all the dry ingredients ahead and store in a ziplock bag. "Thank you, thank you very much ..."

2 cups all-purpose baking mix (such as Bisquick)

1 cup whole milk

½ teaspoon ground cinnamon

¼ teaspoon ground nutmeg

2 large eggs, lightly beaten

1 cup pure maple syrup

½ cup crunchy peanut butter

2 tablespoons salted butter

5 medium-sized ripe bananas

1. Heat a camping stove to medium-high (about 375° to 400°F). Stir together the baking mix, milk, cinnamon, nutmeg, and eggs in a large bowl until blended and smooth.

2. Preheat a cast-iron griddle on the camping stove 8 minutes. Lightly grease the griddle. Pour about ¼ cup batter for each pancake onto the hot griddle, and cook, in batches, until small bubbles appear on the surface. Turn and cook until puffy and cooked through, 1 to 2 minutes. Keep the cooked pancakes warm. Reduce the camping stove heat to medium (about 350° to 375°F).

3. Stir together the maple syrup, peanut butter, and butter in a small saucepan on the camping stove. Cook, stirring gently, just until the peanut butter and butter are melted and blended, 2 to 3 minutes.

4. Place one pancake on a serving plate. Slice one banana; arrange one-third of the slices on top of the pancake, and drizzle with about 1½ tablespoons peanut butter syrup. Repeat the layers twice, ending with the peanut butter syrup. Repeat the process with the remaining pancakes, bananas, and peanut butter syrup.

S'MORES FRENCH TOAST SANDWICHES

HANDS-ON: 15 MINUTES | **TOTAL:** 15 MINUTES | SERVES 4

You'll be the hit of the campsite with everyone's favorite campsite dessert served at breakfast. If cooking for a crowd, keep the finished sandwiches wrapped in foil. This recipe is best served the first morning, while the French bread is still fresh.

1 French bread loaf
½ cup hazelnut-chocolate spread (such as Nutella)
8 regular-sized marshmallows
4 graham crackers (1 sheet)
6 large eggs
½ cup half-and-half
½ teaspoon ground cinnamon
2 tablespoons vegetable oil, divided
1 cup pure maple syrup (optional)

1. Heat a camping stove to medium-high (about 375° to 400°F), or fit a grilling grate over the direct heat of glowing embers. Cut the bread loaf diagonally into 8 (½- to ¾-inch) slices. Spread one side of each bread slice with 1 tablespoon hazelnut-chocolate spread. Top each of four slices with 2 marshmallows and 1 graham cracker. Cover with the remaining bread slices, hazelnut-chocolate spread side down.

2. Whisk together the eggs, half-and-half, and cinnamon in a shallow dish.

3. Heat 1 tablespoon of the vegetable oil in a large nonstick skillet on the camping stove or grilling grate. Dip each sandwich in the egg mixture, coating both sides. Add 2 sandwiches to hot oil in skillet, and cook until the bread is golden brown and cooked through, 2 to 3 minutes per side. (Adjust the heat to prevent excessive browning, if necessary.) Repeat with the remaining 1 tablespoon oil and two sandwiches. Serve with maple syrup, if desired.

APPLE-CINNAMON FRENCH TOAST STRATA

HANDS-ON: 20 MINUTES | **TOTAL:** 2 HOURS, 50 MINUTES | SERVES 8

Save yourself some time and mix everything the night before. Wake up with the sun and have this ready by the time the rest of your camp rises for the day.

1 (8-ounce) package cream cheese, softened
⅓ cup pure maple syrup
2 teaspoons vanilla extract
1 teaspoon ground cinnamon
½ teaspoon table salt
¼ teaspoon ground nutmeg
12 large eggs, lightly beaten
2 cups whole milk
1 (15- to 16-ounce) French bread loaf, cut into 1-inch cubes
1 cup roughly chopped Braeburn apple (about 1 medium)
½ cup chopped toasted pecans
Powdered sugar
Pure maple syrup

1. Line a 9-inch springform pan with heavy-duty aluminum foil, lining all the way to the top edge of the pan. Lightly grease bottom and sides of foil with cooking spray.

2. Whisk together the cream cheese and maple syrup in a large bowl until combined; whisk in the vanilla, cinnamon, salt, and nutmeg. Whisk in eggs until combined; whisk in the milk. Add the bread cubes; stir to coat. Stir in apple and pecans, and let stand at least 30 minutes.

3. Heat a camping stove to medium-low (about 300° to 325°F), or fit a grilling grate over the direct heat of partially glowing embers. Cut 6 (18-inch) squares of foil; crumple each foil square into a 1½- to 2-inch ball. Arrange the foil balls on bottom of a 7½-quart cast-iron Dutch oven; cover with lid. Preheat on the camping stove or a grilling grate directly over the heat source 10 minutes.

4. Pour the bread cube mixture into the prepared springform pan. Place the springform pan on top of the foil balls in the preheated Dutch oven. Coat a large sheet of foil with cooking spray, and place over the top of the Dutch oven, coated side down. Press the foil around the top edge to tightly seal, and cover with the lid. Bake until a knife inserted into the center comes out clean, about 2 hours. Let stand 10 minutes. Remove the sides of the pan; remove the foil from the sides of the strata. Cut into wedges; lightly sprinkle with powdered sugar, and serve with maple syrup.

DRINKS, SNACKS & APPS

BLUEBERRY-CITRUS MULE

HANDS-ON: 5 MINUTES | **TOTAL:** 5 MINUTES | SERVES 6

Don't worry about giving this to the kids—ginger "beer" is not actually beer at all. There is no alcohol in this delicious drink. (Unless, of course, you decide to add some yourself. We won't tell.)

1 pint blueberries (about 2 cups)
½ cup (4 ounces) grapefruit juice
4 (12-ounce) bottles ginger beer
Grapefruit peel strips or twists (optional)

Combine the blueberries and grapefruit juice in a large pitcher. Mash the blueberries until almost all the juices are released. Add the ginger beer; stir to combine. Serve over ice. Garnish with the grapefruit peel strips, if desired.

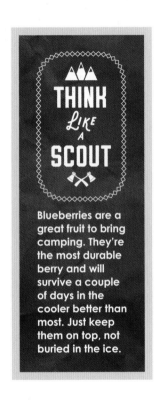

THINK *Like A* SCOUT

Blueberries are a great fruit to bring camping. They're the most durable berry and will survive a couple of days in the cooler better than most. Just keep them on top, not buried in the ice.

BLOODY BARRY

HANDS-ON: 5 MINUTES | **TOTAL:** 5 MINUTES | SERVES 6

Who says you can't have beer in the morning? This take on a Bloody Mary uses beer instead of vodka. Go ahead, crack one open and say hello to the day. If you premeasure and mix the Worcestershire, lemon juice, celery salt, and pepper, you can serve these in a snap even on a bleary-eyed morning.

4 (12-ounce) bottles pale ale beer
2 cups tomato juice
2 teaspoons Worcestershire sauce
1 teaspoon fresh lemon juice (from ½ lemon)
¼ teaspoon celery salt
¼ teaspoon black pepper
4 dashes of hot sauce
Celery stalks (optional)

Stir together all the ingredients in a large pitcher. Serve over ice and, if desired, with celery stalks.

ROY ROGERS

HANDS-ON: 5 MINUTES | **TOTAL:** 5 MINUTES | SERVES 2

Traditionally, this mocktail is made with cola, but the roasty flavor of root beer takes the drink to a whole new level.

2 (12-ounce) bottles root beer or cream soda
¼ cup (2 ounces) maraschino cherry juice
1 tablespoon fresh lime juice (from 1 lime)
Maraschino cherries, stemmed
Lime wedges

Stir together the root beer, cherry juice, and lime juice in a small pitcher; add the cherries, and serve over ice. Garnish with the lime wedges.

THINK LIKE A SCOUT

Normally block ice is better for a cooler than cube ice because it lasts longer, but do bring along some cube ice, too, for cooling drinks. Double-bag it so you don't have to worry about any dairy or meat juices seeping into it.

BEER-RITA

HANDS-ON: 5 MINUTES | **TOTAL:** 5 MINUTES | SERVES 6

With hardy limes as the only fresh produce in this recipe, it's an ideal drink to serve the last evening of your trip.

4 (12-ounce) bottles Mexican lager beer (such as Bohemia Pilsner)
¾ cup (6 ounces) tequila
¾ cup (6 ounces) orange liqueur
6 tablespoons (3 ounces) sweetened lime juice (such as Rose's)
Lime wedges

Stir together the beer, tequila, orange liqueur, and lime juice in a large pitcher. Serve over ice. Garnish with the lime wedges.

THINK *Like* **A SCOUT**

Although it's smart to freeze anything you can before packing your cooler, this definitely does not apply to any carbonated drinks like beer. Consider yourself warned.

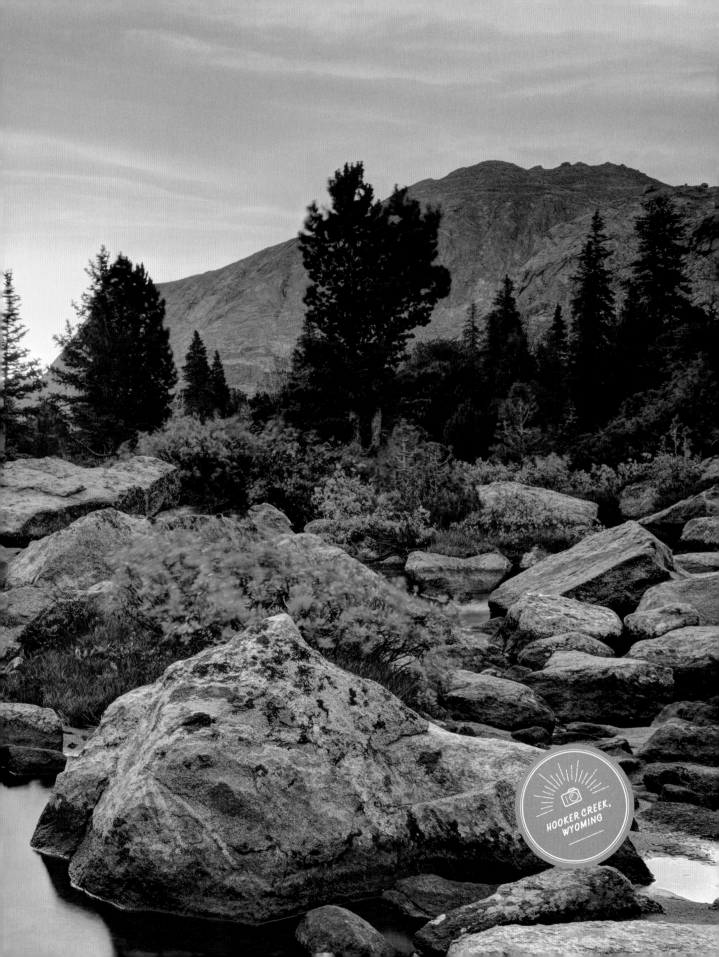

HOOKER CREEK,
WYOMING

SRIRACHA BEEF JERKY

HANDS-ON: 20 MINUTES | **TOTAL:** 9 HOURS, 20 MINUTES | SERVES 16

Jerky is a perfect snack to have on hand when camping, since it requires no refrigeration and is high in protein. This should be made prior to leaving for your camping trip.

2 pounds flank steak, trimmed
½ cup soy sauce
¼ cup packed dark brown sugar
3 tablespoons Sriracha chili sauce
2 tablespoons sesame oil
2 tablespoons tahini (sesame paste)
2 teaspoons grated peeled fresh ginger
2 teaspoons black pepper

1. Pat the steak dry with paper towels. Cover tightly with plastic wrap; place on a baking sheet, and freeze until almost firm, 1 to 2 hours. (Do not freeze steak solid.)

2. Combine the soy sauce, brown sugar, Sriracha, sesame oil, tahini, ginger, and pepper in a large ziplock plastic freezer bag.

3. Cut the meat in half horizontally, making two thin slabs of steak. Slice the meat against the grain into ¼-inch strips. Add to the ziplock bag with marinade; toss to coat. Seal the bag, and refrigerate 3 to 24 hours, turning occasionally.

4. Let the meat stand at room temperature in the bag 1 hour before baking. Preheat the oven to 175°F. Line two rimmed baking sheets with aluminum foil; fit each baking sheet with a wire rack sprayed with cooking spray. Remove the meat strips from the marinade, draining and blotting the excess marinade. Arrange the strips on the prepared racks, leaving about ¼ inch between each strip.

5. Bake in the preheated oven until the meat strips are completely dry, very dark in color, and break apart (depending on the desired degree of chewiness) when gently bent, 4 to 5 hours.

MIXED FRUIT–BASIL ROLL-UPS

HANDS-ON: 35 MINUTES | **TOTAL:** 5 HOURS, 45 MINUTES | SERVES 6

These roll-ups are a great way to get a couple of servings of fruit when you're on the go, and they're a good source of natural sugars to keep you going! Raspberries, strawberries, blackberries, and basil won't last long in the cooler, so this is a great way to bring them along in a more durable form. Make this prior to leaving for the trip. Choose any mixture of berries you like, or use only your favorite.

4 cups mixed berries (such as blueberries, raspberries, strawberries, or blackberries)
¼ cup water
¼ cup granulated sugar
2 teaspoons fresh lemon juice (from ½ lemon)
1 large basil sprig

1. Preheat the oven to 175°F. Combine the berries and water in a 3-quart saucepan over medium heat. Bring to a simmer; cover and cook until the berries are softened, about 8 minutes. Mash the berries with a potato masher or fork. Add the sugar, lemon juice, and basil sprig. Bring the mixture to a simmer, uncovered, and cook, stirring occasionally, until the mixture is thickened, about 10 minutes. Remove and discard the basil sprig.

2. Process the fruit mixture in a blender until smooth. Pour the mixture through a wire-mesh strainer over a bowl; discard the seeds.

3. Line a large rimmed baking sheet with plastic wrap; pour the fruit puree on the plastic wrap, and spread into a (⅛-inch-thick) 15- x 11-inch rectangle.

4. Bake in the preheated oven until the surface of the fruit mixture is dull and no longer soft or sticky to the touch, 5 to 6 hours. Let cool 10 minutes. Cut off and discard any brittle edges. Leave the baked fruit mixture on the plastic wrap; cut in half lengthwise. Cut each half crosswise into thirds to make 6 pieces. Roll each piece up in the plastic wrap, and store in an airtight container at room temperature. If storing for longer than one week, store in the refrigerator or freezer.

SWEET-SAVORY GRANOLA BARS

HANDS-ON: 10 MINUTES | **TOTAL:** 1 HOUR, 40 MINUTES | SERVES 20

These whole-grain, wholesome granola bars will satisfy even the pickiest eater. They're sure to relieve those midday hunger pangs. It is preferable to make these before the trip to have on hand, but you can use a covered grill as an oven to solidify the bars.

2 cups uncooked regular rolled oats
½ cup uncooked whole-grain amaranth
⅔ cup raisins
½ cup roasted, salted almonds
¼ cup roasted, salted pumpkin seeds (pepitas)
½ cup almond butter
¼ cup packed dark brown sugar
¼ cup honey
2 ounces (¼ cup) salted butter
1 tablespoon Worcestershire sauce

1. Preheat the oven to 350°F. Spread the oats and amaranth in an even layer on a large rimmed baking sheet. Bake in the preheated oven until lightly golden, about 15 minutes, stirring after 7 minutes. Transfer to a large bowl; add the raisins, almonds, and pumpkin seeds.

2. Stir together the almond butter, brown sugar, honey, butter, and Worcestershire in a medium saucepan over medium heat; cook, stirring often, until the butter and sugar melt and the mixture begins to bubble, about 6 minutes.

3. Pour the almond butter mixture over the grains and nuts in large bowl; toss to coat.

4. Line a large rimmed baking sheet with parchment paper. Spread the granola mixture on the parchment; press the mixture into a 12- x 10-inch rectangle. Bake in the preheated oven until golden brown and crisp around the edges, about 15 minutes. Cool completely, about 1 hour. (Granola bars will harden as they cool.) Cut into 20 (3- x 2-inch) rectangles, and wrap individually in plastic wrap or aluminum foil for easy lunch and snack packing.

MAPLE-BACON-PECAN POPCORN BALLS

HANDS-ON: 45 MINUTES | **TOTAL:** 45 MINUTES | SERVES 12

This tasty snack is perfect for eating around the campfire while listening to ghost stories. Prepare these balls prior to leaving for your trip. Feel free to use 8 cups of your favorite brand of plain, popped corn, instead of popping your own.

2 tablespoons canola oil

⅓ cup popcorn kernels

4 bacon slices

⅓ cup pecan halves, toasted and chopped

⅓ cup cashews, toasted and chopped

1 cup granulated sugar

½ cup pure maple syrup

¼ cup water

½ teaspoon sea salt

1 teaspoon vanilla extract

1. Heat the oil in a Dutch oven over medium-high. Add one popcorn kernel; cover the Dutch oven and wait for the kernel to pop. Once the kernel pops, add the remaining kernels; cover and cook, shaking the Dutch oven often, until the popping begins to slow, 2 to 3 minutes. Remove from the heat, and let stand until the popping stops, about 1 minute. Transfer the popcorn to a large bowl.

2. Return the Dutch oven to medium. Add the bacon slices, and cook until crisp, about 8 minutes, turning once. Drain on paper towels, reserving 1 tablespoon drippings. Crumble the bacon. Add the bacon, pecans, and cashews to the popcorn.

3. Stir together the sugar, maple syrup, water, salt, and 1 tablespoon reserved bacon drippings in a medium saucepan. Bring to a boil over medium-high, stirring often to dissolve the sugar. Cook over medium-high until a candy thermometer inserted in the mixture registers 275°F, about 12 minutes, swirling the pan occasionally. Remove from the heat; stir in the vanilla.

4. Immediately drizzle the hot syrup over the popcorn mixture while stirring with a silicone spatula coated with cooking spray. (Syrup won't stick to it.) Carefully form the mixture into 12 (2½- to 3-inch) balls (about ⅔ cup popcorn mixture per ball), being careful not to compact too tightly. Store in an airtight container up to 2 days. To make them easy to hand out for snacks, put each ball into a paper sandwich bag to keep them from sticking together, and store them in an airtight container.

THINK *LIKE A* **SCOUT**

While you're at it, fry some extra bacon until it's about half done, then wrap it in paper towels and store it in a ziplock bag. When you're at the campsite, you can finish cooking the bacon for an easy, hot side item for breakfast.

OLYMPIC NATIONAL
PARK, WASHINGTON

CANDIED BACON–WRAPPED SMOKIES

HANDS-ON: 15 MINUTES | **TOTAL:** 15 MINUTES | SERVES 7

These yummy fireside treats will disappear quickly. Feel free to double the recipe!

¼ cup packed brown sugar
1 tablespoon yellow or Dijon mustard
½ teaspoon Sriracha chili sauce or cayenne pepper
1 (16-ounce) package cocktail-sized smoked beef sausages,
   drained and rinsed
8 bacon slices, cut crosswise into fourths
Honey or pure maple syrup (optional)

1. Heat a camping stove or grill to medium-high (about 375° to 400°F), or fit a grilling grate over the direct heat of glowing embers. Combine the brown sugar, mustard, and Sriracha in a small bowl; set aside.

2. Wrap each sausage with one bacon piece; secure with a wooden pick, if needed. Place the wrapped sausages on the camping stove or grilling grate directly over the heat source, and grill until browned on one side, about 3 minutes. Turn and brush with the brown sugar mixture; grill until browned, about 3 minutes. Repeat until the wrapped sausages are thoroughly coated and the bacon is crisp but not burnt, 1 to 2 minutes. Serve drizzled with honey or maple syrup, if desired.

BLISTERED TOMATOES WITH RICOTTA AND PESTO

HANDS-ON: 20 MINUTES | **TOTAL:** 30 MINUTES | SERVES 6

Even though this pesto can be easily made on a cutting board, making it before the trip means you don't need to worry about the herbs' tendency to go black and mushy in the cooler. Store-bought, good-quality basil pesto would work well in a pinch.

¼ cup roasted, salted whole almonds

2 garlic cloves

1 cup firmly packed fresh basil leaves

½ cup firmly packed fresh flat-leaf parsley leaves

½ teaspoon grated lemon zest plus 1 teaspoon fresh juice (from 1 lemon)

6 tablespoons extra-virgin olive oil, divided

1 teaspoon kosher salt, divided

2 pints cherry tomatoes

½ teaspoon black pepper

1 pound fresh ricotta cheese

1 baguette, torn and toasted

1. Roughly chop the almonds and garlic. Add the basil and parsley; continue to roughly chop until the pieces are uniform in size. Spoon the mixture into a bowl; stir in the zest, juice, ¼ cup of the oil, and ½ teaspoon of the salt. Store the pesto in an airtight container up to 1 week.

2. Heat a camping stove to medium (about 350° to 375°F), or fit a grilling grate over the direct heat of glowing embers. Preheat a 12-inch cast-iron skillet on the camping stove or grilling grate directly over the heat source 5 minutes. Toss together the tomatoes, pepper, and remaining 2 tablespoons oil and ½ teaspoon salt; add the mixture to the hot skillet. Cook, stirring occasionally, until the tomatoes are blistered and charred, 8 to 10 minutes. Serve with the pesto, ricotta, and torn baguette.

GETTING

GEARED UP

A camping toaster may sound like an absurd first-timer's indulgence. But it's actually a simple, inexpensive metal frame that sits on your camping stove and allows you to prop up bread to toast without burning. It will come in handy with this recipe: To crisp up a baguette that's been bagged for a day or two, just slice it into 6-inch lengths, cut the pieces in half lengthwise, and toast them a bit before tearing into pieces for serving.

CHICKEN ENCHILADA NACHOS

HANDS-ON: 10 MINUTES | **TOTAL:** 20 MINUTES | SERVES 6

You can make enchilada sauce and store it in an airtight container in the cooler if you like, but a store-bought version works just fine in this recipe. Picking apart the chicken at home will save you cooler space (and a greasy mess at the site). Avocados don't do well in a cooler but ripen quickly in a hot car. Buy yours a bit unripe and leave them in the car a few hours after unloading if needed.

2 cups shredded cooked chicken (from 1 rotisserie chicken)

1 (10-ounce) can red enchilada sauce

2 tablespoons sour cream plus more for serving

1 (13-ounce) package tortilla chips

1 (15-ounce) can black or pinto beans, drained and rinsed

1 (8-ounce) package preshredded Mexican 4-cheese blend

1 small ripe avocado, diced

1 cup shredded red or green cabbage

Chopped fresh cilantro

Lime wedges

Heat a camping stove or grill to medium (about 350° to 375°F), or fit a grilling grate over the direct heat of glowing embers. Toss together the shredded chicken, enchilada sauce, and sour cream in a large bowl. Spread half of the chips in a 12-inch cast-iron skillet; top with half of the chicken mixture, half of the beans, and half of the cheese. Repeat the layers once. Cover the skillet with aluminum foil, and place on the grate. Grill until the cheese melts, 10 to 15 minutes. Top with the diced avocado, cabbage, and cilantro. Serve with the lime wedges.

FRENCH ONION SOUP DIP

HANDS-ON: 20 MINUTES | **TOTAL:** 30 MINUTES | SERVES 6

This delicious dip is made in aluminum foil—cleanup couldn't be easier! Serve with bagged bagel crisps or grilled bread. Caramelize the onions at home before you leave, and store in an airtight container in your cooler until ready to use.

1 (8-ounce) package cream cheese
½ cup mayonnaise
½ cup Caramelized Onions
4 ounces Gruyère cheese, diced (about 1 cup)
½ teaspoon black pepper
Bagel crisps or grilled bread

1. Heat a camping stove or grill to medium-high (about 375° to 400°F), or fit a grilling grate over the direct heat of glowing embers. Cut or tear a 16- x 14-inch rectangle of heavy-duty aluminum foil. Place the cream cheese in the center of the foil; top with the mayonnaise, onions, and Gruyère. Bring the long sides up and over the cheese mixture; double-fold the top and sides of the foil, and tightly seal.

2. Place the foil packet on the camping stove or grilling grate, and cook until the cheeses are melted, 10 to 15 minutes. Remove from the heat; open the foil, and stir to combine. Sprinkle with the pepper. Serve immediately with the bagel crisps or grilled bread.

CARAMELIZED ONIONS

HANDS-ON: 15 MINUTES | **TOTAL:** 1 HOUR | MAKES 2 CUPS

Heat 2 tablespoons olive oil in a medium skillet over medium-low. Add 4 cups thinly sliced sweet onions (about 16 ounces) and 1½ teaspoons chopped fresh thyme; cook, stirring occasionally, until the onions are very soft and golden brown, about 35 minutes. Add 1 tablespoon apple cider vinegar and ¼ teaspoon kosher salt, stirring and scraping the browned bits from the bottom of the skillet. Remove the skillet from heat, and cool the onions to room temperature, about 10 minutes. Roughly chop the onions, and store in an airtight container for up to 1 week.

CHORI-QUESO

HANDS-ON: 15 MINUTES | **TOTAL:** 20 MINUTES | SERVES 6

This should take you back to your favorite Mexican restaurant. If you use diced dry-cured Spanish chorizo, you can skip the browning step. Simply put all the ingredients in a foil packet and grill until the cheese melts.

8 ounces fresh Mexican chorizo, casing removed
2 (4-ounce) cans diced green chiles, undrained
1½ tablespoons minced garlic
1 (8-ounce) package cream cheese, softened
½ cup whole milk
8 ounces Monterey Jack cheese, shredded (about 2 cups)
Cilantro leaves (optional)
Jalapeño slices (optional)
Tortilla chips

Heat a camping stove or grill to medium (about 350° to 375°F), or fit a grilling grate over the direct heat of glowing embers. Place a 10-inch cast-iron skillet on the grate, and heat until hot, about 5 minutes. Add the chorizo, and cook, stirring often to crumble, until browned and cooked through, about 8 minutes. Add the green chiles and garlic; cook until fragrant, about 1 minute. Add the cream cheese and milk; cook, stirring constantly, until melted and thickened, about 2 minutes. Remove from the heat; fold in the Monterey Jack, and stir until melted, about 2 minutes. Sprinkle with the cilantro and jalapeño slices, if desired. Serve immediately with the tortilla chips.

THINK *Like* **A SCOUT**

Save this recipe, made up of packable and durable ingredients, for late in the trip after your produce and fresh bread have gone south.

CAMPING PEAR, BRIE, AND ARUGULA QUESADILLAS

HANDS-ON: 15 MINUTES | **TOTAL:** 15 MINUTES | SERVES 4

This gourmet quesadilla pairs perfectly with a crisp cider or white wine. You may substitute plain Dijon mustard for the whole-grain version.

THINK Like A SCOUT

Fragile items like the arugula and pears in this recipe don't fare well in the cooler. After washing and drying them, wrap them in paper towels and put them in at least a ziplock—better yet an airtight plastic container. Keep them above the ice at the top of the cooler. Pears are even better bought a bit unripe and kept outside the cooler.

1½ tablespoons whole-grain Dijon mustard
1 tablespoon honey
½ teaspoon black pepper
4 (8-inch) flour tortillas
1 tablespoon canola oil or cooking spray
10 ounces Brie, rind removed, cut into ¼-inch-thick slices
8 ounces Bosc pears (about 2 small pears), thinly sliced
2 ounces arugula (about 2 cups)

1. Heat a camping stove or grill to medium (about 350° to 375°F), or fit a grilling grate over the direct heat of glowing embers. Combine the mustard, honey, and pepper in a small bowl. Brush one side of tortillas with the oil or spray with the cooking spray; spread the second side of each tortilla with 1½ teaspoons of the mustard mixture.

2. Place each tortilla, oiled side down, on the camping stove or grilling grate directly over the heat source. Arrange ¼ of the cheese slices evenly on half of each tortilla; grill until the cheese begins to melt, about 1 minute. Arrange the pears and arugula evenly over the cheese. Using a spatula, fold each tortilla in half to cover the filling, pressing gently to adhere. Grill until the arugula wilts, the tortillas are browned and crisp, and the cheese is melted, 1 to 2 minutes per side. Cut each quesadilla into 2 wedges.

SPARKS LAKE,
OREGON

Chapter Three

SANDWICHES & SALADS

LOADED CAMP CHEDDAR BURGERS WITH CHIVE CREAM

HANDS-ON: 30 MINUTES | **TOTAL:** 30 MINUTES | SERVES 6

Dive into this delicious, well-seasoned, and slightly spicy burger, balanced by the cool chive cream, sweet onions, and rich Cheddar. Blending the leanness of sirloin with the fatty, rich flavor of chuck creates the perfect burger.

1 pound ground sirloin
½ pound ground chuck
2 tablespoons finely chopped pickled jalapeño chiles
2 garlic cloves, minced
1½ teaspoons kosher salt
¼ cup sour cream
¼ cup mayonnaise
2 tablespoons thinly sliced fresh chives
1 tablespoon fresh lemon juice
2 tablespoons olive oil
6 (¾-ounce) Cheddar cheese slices
1 large sweet onion, thinly sliced
6 hamburger buns, toasted
Lettuce leaves
Tomato slices
Home Fries

1. Heat a camping stove to medium (350° to 375°F), or fit a grilling grate over the direct heat of glowing embers. Combine the ground sirloin, ground chuck, pickled jalapeños, garlic, and salt in a medium bowl. Gently shape the mixture into 6 (4-inch) patties. Stir together the sour cream, mayonnaise, chives, and lemon juice in a small bowl, and set aside.

2. Heat the oil in a 12-inch cast-iron skillet on the camping stove or grilling grate directly over the heat source; add 3 patties to the skillet, cover, and cook until the beef is no longer pink in the center, 4 to 5 minutes per side. Top each patty with 1 cheese slice, and remove to a platter. Loosely cover with heavy-duty aluminum foil. Repeat the procedure with the remaining patties and cheese slices. Reserve the drippings in the skillet.

3. Add the onions to the hot drippings in the skillet, and cook, stirring often, until tender, 6 to 8 minutes. Serve the patties on hamburger buns with the onions, lettuce, tomato, and sour cream mixture. Serve with Home Fries.

HOME FRIES

HANDS-ON: 15 MINUTES | **TOTAL:** 45 MINUTES | SERVES 6

Heat a camping stove to medium (350° to 375°F), or fit a grilling grate over
the direct heat of glowing embers. Dice 3 russet potatoes (about 1½ pounds).
Bring potatoes, 1 teaspoon table salt, and water to cover to a boil in a small
cast-iron Dutch oven; boil until fork-tender, 10 to 15 minutes. Drain; spread
on paper towels, and cool 20 minutes. Melt 1 tablespoon salted butter with
2 tablespoons olive oil in a 10-inch cast-iron skillet on the camping stove or
grilling grate directly over the heat source; add the potatoes, and cook until
golden brown and crisp, 10 to 15 minutes, stirring once. Sprinkle with ½
teaspoon table salt and ¼ teaspoon black pepper.

GREEN CHILE BURGERS WITH MONTEREY JACK AND CUMIN-LIME MAYO

HANDS-ON: 25 MINUTES | **TOTAL:** 25 MINUTES | SERVES 6

Cooking these burgers in a cast-iron skillet creates a wonderful even crust on the outside. Look for the chopped green chiles in the international aisle of your local grocery store.

1½ pounds ground round
1 (4.5-ounce) can chopped green chiles, drained
1 tablespoon chili powder
½ teaspoon kosher salt
½ cup mayonnaise
1 tablespoon fresh lime juice
2 teaspoons ground cumin
2 tablespoons olive oil, divided
6 (¾-ounce) Monterey Jack cheese slices
6 sesame seed hamburger buns, toasted
1 cup loosely packed fresh cilantro leaves

1. Heat a camping stove or grill to medium-high (about 375° to 400°F), or fit a grilling grate over the direct heat of glowing embers. Gently combine the beef, chiles, chili powder, and salt in a medium bowl. Gently shape the mixture into 6 (4-inch) patties. Stir together the mayonnaise, lime juice, and cumin in a small bowl; set aside.

2. Heat 1 tablespoon of the oil in a 12-inch cast-iron skillet on the camping stove or grilling grate directly over the heat source. Add 3 patties; cook, covered, until the beef is no longer pink in the center, 4 to 5 minutes per side. Top each patty with 1 cheese slice; remove to a plate, and loosely cover with heavy-duty aluminum foil. Repeat with the remaining 1 tablespoon oil and 3 patties.

3. Spread the mayonnaise mixture evenly on the cut sides of the toasted buns. Top the bottom halves of the buns with the patties, cilantro, and the top halves of the buns.

PIGGY BURGERS WITH BACON, PEACHES, AND BASIL

HANDS-ON: 30 MINUTES | **TOTAL:** 30 MINUTES | SERVES 6

This is a pork flavor explosion! The well-seasoned ground pork patties cooked in bacon fat are a camping treat. The tangy goat cheese and sweet fresh peaches round out and balance the rich porcine flavor.

1½ pounds ground pork
1 teaspoon kosher salt
½ teaspoon black pepper
6 thick-cut bacon slices
4 ounces goat cheese, softened (about 1 cup)
6 hamburger buns
2 medium-sized peaches, thinly sliced
Basil leaves

1. Heat a camping stove to medium (about 350° to 375°F), or fit a grilling grate over the direct heat of glowing embers. Combine the pork, salt, and pepper. Gently shape into 6 (4-inch) patties.

2. Cook the bacon in a 12-inch cast-iron skillet on the camping stove or grilling grate directly over the heat source until crisp, 8 to 10 minutes. Remove the bacon, and drain on paper towels, reserving 3 tablespoons drippings in the skillet.

3. Add the patties to the hot drippings in the skillet, and cook, covered with a lid, until no longer pink in the center, 4 to 5 minutes per side. Top the patties with the goat cheese, and serve on the hamburger buns with the bacon, peach slices, and basil leaves.

CAROLINA-STYLE CHICKEN BURGERS WITH CREAMY CHIPOTLE SLAW

HANDS-ON: 20 MINUTES | **TOTAL:** 20 MINUTES | SERVES 6

The chicken patties are very wet and sticky, but don't fret; they are tender and moist, as a result. We found it's best to cook them on a grill pan instead of the grill since the patties are more delicate than traditional beef burgers.

2 pounds ground chicken
⅓ cup mayonnaise
1 tablespoon whole-grain Dijon mustard
1 teaspoon kosher salt
½ teaspoon black pepper
6 sesame seed hamburger buns
Creamy Chipotle Slaw
Dill pickle slices

1. Heat a camping stove or grill to medium (about 350° to 375°F), or fit a grilling grate over the direct heat of glowing embers. Gently combine the ground chicken, mayonnaise, mustard, salt, and pepper in a large bowl. Shape the mixture into 6 patties.

2. Grill the patties in a grill pan on the camping stove or grilling grate directly over the heat source until a meat thermometer inserted in the thickest portion registers 165°F, about 7 minutes per side. Grill the buns until toasted, about 1 minute per side. Place a patty on the bottom half of each bun. Top with Creamy Chipotle Slaw and pickles, and cover with the top of the bun.

CREAMY CHIPOTLE SLAW

HANDS-ON: 15 MINUTES | **TOTAL:** 30 MINUTES | SERVES 6

Whisk together ½ cup mayonnaise, 2 tablespoons apple cider vinegar, 2 teaspoons granulated sugar, ¾ teaspoon ground chipotle chile powder, ½ teaspoon kosher salt, and ½ teaspoon black pepper in a large bowl. Add ½ small savoy cabbage head, shredded or finely chopped; 1 large celery stalk, chopped; and ½ cup grated carrot, and toss to coat. Let stand 15 minutes before serving, tossing occasionally.

PORTOBELLO MUSHROOM CHEESEBURGERS

HANDS-ON: 20 MINUTES | **TOTAL:** 20 MINUTES | SERVES 4

The hearty portobello mushrooms and rich Havarti complement each other nicely in this vegetarian-friendly burger. The horseradish sauce lends a perfect kick. You can make it ahead, if you like.

8 portobello mushrooms, stems and gills removed, tops scored
¼ cup plus 2 tablespoons olive oil, divided
4 Havarti cheese slices
½ teaspoon kosher salt
½ teaspoon black pepper
4 kaiser rolls
½ cup Creamy Horseradish Sauce
1 cup loosely packed arugula

1. Heat a camping stove or grill to medium (about 375° to 400°F), or fit a grilling grate over the direct heat of glowing embers. Brush the mushrooms with ¼ cup of the olive oil.

2. Place the mushrooms on the camping stove or grilling grate, and cover with a 13- x 9-inch disposable aluminum baking pan. Grill until tender and lightly charred, about 5 minutes. Place 1 cheese slice on each of 4 mushrooms; top with remaining 4 mushrooms. Grill until the cheese is melted, about 1 minute. Sprinkle with the salt and pepper.

3. Meanwhile, split the kaiser rolls, and brush with the remaining 2 tablespoons olive oil. Grill until toasted, about 1 minute per side. Spread 1 tablespoon Creamy Horseradish Sauce over each roll half. Place 1 mushroom stack and ¼ cup arugula on the bottom halves of the rolls; cover with the top halves, and serve immediately.

CREAMY HORSERADISH SAUCE

HANDS-ON: 5 MINUTES | **TOTAL:** 5 MINUTES | MAKES ABOUT ¾ CUP

Stir together ½ cup sour cream, ¼ cup plain Greek yogurt, 1½ tablespoons prepared horseradish, 1½ teaspoons chopped fresh chives, ½ teaspoon white wine vinegar, ½ teaspoon black pepper, and ¼ teaspoon kosher salt.

FIRESIDE SLOPPY JOES

HANDS-ON: 25 MINUTES | **TOTAL:** 25 MINUTES | SERVES 4

Have plenty of paper towels on hand for this homemade version of this classic—and aptly named—sandwich.

1 tablespoon unsalted butter
1¼ cups finely chopped yellow onion (from 1 large onion)
¾ cup chopped red bell pepper (from 1 medium pepper)
1 tablespoon minced garlic
1½ pounds ground chuck
1 (10-ounce) can tomato puree
1 cup ketchup
2 tablespoons Worcestershire sauce
1 tablespoon light brown sugar
1 tablespoon chili powder
¾ teaspoon kosher salt
4 sesame seed hamburger buns
Hot sauce (optional)

1. Heat a camping stove or grill to medium-high (about 375° to 400°F).

2. Melt the butter in a 12-inch cast-iron skillet on the camping stove or grilling grate. Add the onion, bell pepper, and garlic to the skillet; cook, stirring occasionally, until softened, about 10 minutes. Remove the vegetables from the skillet. Add the beef to the skillet; cook, stirring often, until the meat crumbles and is no longer pink, about 5 minutes. Return the vegetable mixture to the skillet. Add the tomato puree, ketchup, Worcestershire, sugar, chili powder, and salt; bring to a simmer. Reduce the heat to medium-low (about 300° to 325°F); cover and cook, stirring occasionally, until heated through, about 10 minutes. Divide the mixture evenly among the hamburger buns. Serve with the hot sauce, if desired.

CAMPFIRE-COOKED SAUSAGE-AND-PEPPERS HOAGIES

HANDS-ON: 10 MINUTES | **TOTAL**: 30 MINUTES | SERVES 4

Charred, spicy sausage paired with roasted sweet peppers and onions is a winner through and through. Add slices of provolone to the hoagies for a melty, cheesy option. You can substitute other smoked sausages or bratwurst if you prefer.

If you're cooking over a fire, here's a rule of thumb for checking its heat level: Once the coals are gray, put your hand 4 inches above the grilling grate. If you can't keep it there more than 3 seconds, that's a hot fire. If you can hold it there 3 to 4 seconds, consider it medium, and if you can stay longer than 5 seconds, that's low heat.

4 (4-ounce) spicy Italian sausages
1 large red onion, cut crosswise into 4 (½-inch-thick) slices
1 red bell pepper, cut into ½-inch slices
1 yellow bell pepper, cut into ½-inch slices
1 poblano chile, cut into ½-inch slices
1 tablespoon extra-virgin olive oil
½ cup torn fresh herbs, such as basil and oregano
1 teaspoon kosher salt
½ teaspoon black pepper
4 hoagie rolls, split
8 (¾-ounce) provolone cheese slices (optional)

1. Heat a camping stove or grill to medium-high (about 375° to 400°F), or fit a grilling grate over the direct heat of glowing embers. Place the sausages, onion slices, bell pepper slices, and poblano slices on the grilling grate directly over the heat source; grill, turning occasionally, until charred, about 10 minutes.

2. Tear or cut 4 (18-inch) squares of aluminum foil. Divide the sausages and vegetables evenly among the foil squares. Drizzle evenly with the oil; sprinkle evenly with the herbs, salt, and black pepper. Toss to coat. Gather the edges of each foil sheet into a packet, and crimp to seal. Place the packets on the grill grate; grill until the sausages are cooked through, 10 to 15 minutes.

3. Top the bottom half of each roll with 2 provolone slices, if desired. Divide the sausages and vegetable mixture evenly among the rolls. Top with the top halves of rolls.

GRAND CANYON
NATIONAL PARK,
ARIZONA

GRILLED SHRIMP RÉMOULADE PO'BOYS

HANDS-ON: 10 MINUTES | **TOTAL:** 15 MINUTES | SERVES 6

Look for shrimp that are 16/v20 count—that is, about 16 to 20 shrimp per pound. Impress your crew with an unexpected, zesty meal that can be on the table very quickly if you peel and devein the shrimp at home.

1 cup mayonnaise
¼ cup sliced scallions
2 tablespoons Creole mustard
2 teaspoons grated lime zest plus 2 tablespoons fresh juice
    (from 1 large lime)
½ teaspoon hot sauce
1¼ teaspoons kosher salt, divided
2 pounds raw medium-sized shrimp, peeled and deveined
3 tablespoons olive oil, divided
6 hoagie rolls, split
Chopped romaine lettuce

1. Heat a camping stove or grill to medium (about 350° to 375°F), or fit a grilling grate over the direct heat of glowing embers. Stir together the mayonnaise, scallions, mustard, zest, juice, hot sauce, and ¼ teaspoon of the salt in a medium bowl. Cover and chill until ready to use.

2. Toss the shrimp, 2 tablespoons of the oil, and remaining 1 teaspoon salt in a large bowl. Grill the shrimp on the camping stove or grilling grate directly over the heat source just until they turn pink, 3 to 4 minutes per side.

3. Brush the cut sides of the rolls evenly with the remaining 1 tablespoon oil. Grill, cut sides down, until slightly charred and crispy, about 2 minutes.

4. Spread the cut sides of each roll with about 1 tablespoon rémoulade. Divide the shrimp and lettuce evenly among the bottom halves of the rolls. Cover with the tops of the rolls. Serve with the remaining rémoulade.

SLOPPY COLA JOES

HANDS-ON: 30 MINUTES | **TOTAL:** 30 MINUTES | SERVES 8

These aren't just for kids anymore! This sweet and savory classic comes together with ease after a day of adventure. Substitute any dark soda and top your dog with chopped onion or your favorite coleslaw for crunch and color.

1 medium-sized red onion, thinly sliced
2 tablespoons olive oil
1½ pounds ground sirloin
1 (6-ounce) can tomato paste
1 tablespoon Worcestershire sauce
1 garlic clove, minced
1 (12-ounce) can spicy, fruity cola soft drink (such as Dr Pepper)
½ cup jarred sliced pepperoncini salad peppers
1 teaspoon kosher salt
½ teaspoon cayenne pepper
8 hot dog buns

1. Heat a camping stove or grill to medium-high (about 375° to 400°F), or fit a grilling grate over the direct heat of glowing embers. Cook the onion in hot oil in a 12-inch cast-iron skillet on the camping stove or grilling grate directly over the heat source until the onions are caramel-colored, about 15 minutes.

2. Add the ground sirloin to the skillet, and cook, stirring often, until the meat crumbles and is no longer pink, 5 to 6 minutes.

3. Stir in the tomato paste, Worcestershire sauce, and garlic, and cook, stirring occasionally, until the mixture thickens and the color darkens, 3 to 4 minutes. Stir in the cola, and cook, stirring constantly, until thickened, about 3 minutes. Remove from the heat, and stir in the pepperoncini peppers, salt, and cayenne pepper.

4. Spoon the beef mixture into the buns, and serve immediately.

ROASTED CHICKEN SALAD LOAF

HANDS-ON: 10 MINUTES | **TOTAL:** 15 MINUTES | SERVES 4

Adding fennel to traditional chicken salad elevates the flavor. Make the salad ahead of your camping trip and store it, chilled, in your cooler.

6 cups chopped rotisserie chicken

1 cup mayonnaise

4 scallions, minced

2 celery stalks, diced

3 tablespoons fresh lime juice (from 2 limes)

2 teaspoons ground fennel seeds

1 teaspoon kosher salt

¼ teaspoon black pepper

1 (12-ounce) baguette, cut in half lengthwise

Lettuce leaves (optional)

Tomato slices (optional)

1. Stir together the chicken, mayonnaise, scallions, celery, lime juice, ground fennel, salt, and pepper in a large bowl just until combined.

2. Heat a camping stove or grill to medium (about 350° to 375°F), or fit a grilling grate over the direct heat of glowing embers. Grill the baguette halves, cut sides down, on the grilling grate directly over the heat source until toasted, about 1 minute per side. Spread the bottom half of the baguette with the chicken salad. Top with the lettuce and tomato, if desired. Cover with the top half of the baguette; cut the sandwich into 5-inch pieces.

CHICKEN PANINI WITH GARLIC AND HERBS

HANDS-ON: 15 MINUTES | **TOTAL:** 15 MINUTES | SERVES 6

These Mediterranean panini are ready in a flash. For best results, place something heavy (such as a skillet, brick, or cans of beans) on top of the sandwiches while they cook in the skillet.

2 (4-ounce) containers garlic-and-herb spreadable cheese
12 sourdough bread slices
4 cooked boneless, skinless chicken breasts (about 2 pounds), sliced
1½ cups loosely packed baby spinach
½ cup thinly sliced roasted red bell peppers
2 ounces (¼ cup) salted butter, melted

1. Heat a camping stove or grill to medium (about 350° to 375°F), or fit a grilling grate over the direct heat of glowing embers.

2. Spread the garlic-herb cheese on one side of each bread slice. Layer 6 bread slices with the chicken, spinach, and roasted red peppers; cover the sandwiches with the remaining bread slices. Brush both sides of the sandwiches with the melted butter.

3. Place a 12-inch cast-iron skillet on the camping stove or grilling grate directly over the heat source. Place the sandwiches in the skillet; top with a smaller skillet, or press down with spatula to flatten the sandwiches slightly during cooking. Grill the sandwiches, in batches, until the bread is golden brown and heated throughout and the cheese has melted, about 1 minute per side. Serve immediately.

HANGER STEAK, CHARRED RED ONION, AND BLUE CHEESE FOCACCIA SANDWICHES

HANDS-ON: 20 MINUTES | **TOTAL:** 8 HOURS, 20 MINUTES | SERVES 4

This is the perfect combination of tangy blue cheese, savory beef, and sweet red onion in sandwich form. The blue cheese spread can be made ahead, and the beef can marinate for up to two days.

1½ pounds hanger steak, membrane removed and
    cut crosswise into 4 pieces

3 garlic cloves, smashed

3 rosemary sprigs

3 thyme sprigs

1½ teaspoons kosher salt

½ teaspoon black pepper

3 tablespoons olive oil, divided

4 ounces blue cheese, crumbled (about 1 cup)

2 tablespoons sour cream

2 tablespoons mayonnaise

1 teaspoon red wine vinegar

1 red onion, cut into 4 (½-inch-thick) slices

8 focaccia bread slices

1. Place the steak, garlic, rosemary, thyme, salt, pepper, and 2 tablespoons of the olive oil in a 1-gallon ziplock bag. Seal and massage the seasonings into the meat. Chill 8 to 24 hours, massaging occasionally.

2. Stir together the blue cheese, sour cream, mayonnaise, and vinegar. Set aside.

3. Heat a camping stove or grill to medium (about 350° to 375°F), or fit a grilling grate over the direct heat of glowing embers. Brush the onion slices with the remaining 1 tablespoon olive oil. Grill the onions on the camping stove or grilling grate directly over the heat source until tender and charred, 6 to 8 minutes per side. At the same time, grill the steak until desired degree of doneness is reached, about 5 minutes per side. Let the steak stand 5 minutes; cut across the grain into thin slices.

4. Spread each bread slice with about 1 tablespoon blue cheese mixture. Layer 4 bread slices with about 5 ounces of steak and 1 onion slice. Top with the remaining bread slices, and serve immediately.

GRILLED PORK BÁNH MÌ WITH CUCUMBER-MINT SALAD

HANDS-ON: 10 MINUTES | **TOTAL:** 45 MINUTES | SERVES 4

Enjoy this Vietnamese-style sandwich fireside. The quick pickle salad and spicy mayo pairs perfectly with the smoky grilled pork.

2 cups matchstick carrots
⅓ English cucumber, sliced into thin strips
2 scallions, chopped
3 tablespoons fresh lime juice (from about 2 limes)
¼ cup sesame oil
1½ tablespoons soy sauce
1 tablespoon Asian sweet chili sauce
½ teaspoon black pepper
1 (1½-pound) pork tenderloin
1 large French baguette, cut into 4 pieces, cut in half lengthwise,
    top and bottom scooped out
½ cup loosely packed fresh mint leaves
Spicy Mayo

1. Toss together the carrots, cucumber, scallions, and lime juice in a bowl. Set aside.

2. Heat a camping stove or grill to medium-high (about 375° to 400°F), or fit a grilling grate over the direct heat of glowing embers. Stir together the sesame oil, soy sauce, sweet chili sauce, and black pepper in a small bowl; brush over the pork tenderloin. Grill the tenderloin on the camping stove or grilling grate directly over the heat source until a meat thermometer inserted into the thickest portion registers 155°F, 10 to 12 minutes per side. Remove from the grilling grate, and let stand 10 minutes.

3. Meanwhile, grill the baguette until toasted, about 1 minute on each side. Stir the mint into the carrot-cucumber mixture.

4. Spread 1 tablespoon Spicy Mayo on the cut side of each French bread slice; top 4 bottom bread slices with the sliced pork tenderloin and carrot-cucumber mixture. Cover the sandwiches with the remaining 4 bread slices, and serve immediately.

SPICY MAYO

HANDS-ON: 5 MINUTES | **TOTAL:** 5 MINUTES | MAKES ABOUT ½ CUP

Stir together ½ cup mayonnaise and 2 tablespoons each sambal oelek and dill pickle relish in a small bowl.

THINK LIKE A SCOUT

If bees or wasps are bothering you, try leaving a few extra slices of the cucumber around the table. The insects hate cucumber and tend to steer clear.

SKILLET-PRESSED BACON-AND-PIMIENTO CHEESE SANDWICHES

HANDS-ON: 15 MINUTES | **TOTAL:** 25 MINUTES | SERVES 6

Pimiento cheese is a Southern classic, and once you've had homemade you'll understand why. Paired with smoky bacon and tangy sourdough, this toasty sandwich will keep you satisfied.

1 cup mayonnaise
1 (4-ounce) jar diced pimiento, drained
¼ teaspoon cayenne pepper
8 ounces white extra-sharp Cheddar cheese, shredded
    (about 2 cups)
8 ounces sharp Cheddar cheese, shredded (about 2 cups)
12 sourdough bread slices
12 thick-cut applewood-smoked bacon slices, cooked
2 ounces (¼ cup) salted butter, melted

1. Stir together the mayonnaise, pimiento, and cayenne pepper in a large bowl until blended.

2. Gradually stir the shredded cheeses into the mayonnaise mixture; cover and chill until ready to use.

3. Heat a camping stove or grill to medium (about 350° to 375°F), or fit a grilling grate over the direct heat of glowing embers. Spread about 3 tablespoons of the pimiento cheese on each of 6 bread slices; top each with 2 bacon slices. Cover with the remaining bread slices, and brush both sides of the sandwiches with the melted butter.

4. Place the sandwiches in a 12-inch cast-iron skillet on the camping stove or grilling grate directly over the heat source. Place the sandwiches in the skillet; top with a smaller skillet, or press down with spatula to flatten the sandwiches slightly during cooking. Grill the sandwiches, in batches, until the bread is golden brown and the pimiento cheese melts, 2 to 3 minutes per side. Serve immediately.

MOUNT RAINIER
NATIONAL PARK,
WASHINGTON

CRUNCHY BLACK-AND-BLUE SALAD

HANDS-ON: 25 MINUTES | **TOTAL:** 25 MINUTES | SERVES 4

It's best to let these coffee-crusted steaks (or any steaks for that matter) rest after they come off the heat. The short stand time allows the juices to redistribute in the meat instead of running all over the cutting board, which happens if you slice into it too soon. Crumbled kettle-cooked potato chips are a fun alternative to croutons.

2 teaspoons kosher salt

1½ teaspoons black pepper

1 teaspoon ground coffee beans

2 (12-ounce) New York strip steaks

¼ cup plus 1 tablespoon olive oil, divided

2 tablespoons balsamic vinegar

2 teaspoons honey

1 teaspoon Dijon mustard

2 cups cherry tomato halves

2 romaine lettuce heads, chopped

¾ cup thinly sliced red onion (from 1 onion)

¾ cup crumbled kettle-cooked potato chips

2 ounces blue cheese, crumbled (about ½ cup)

1. Heat a camping stove or grill to medium-high (about 375° to 400°F), or fit a grilling grate over the direct heat of glowing embers.

2. Combine the salt, pepper, and coffee. Rub the steaks with 1 tablespoon of the oil; sprinkle with the spice mixture, pressing to adhere. Place the steaks on the camping stove or grilling grate directly over the heat source, and grill to about medium-rare, 7 to 8 minutes per side. Let rest on a cutting board 5 minutes. Thinly slice across the grain.

3. Whisk together the vinegar, honey, mustard, and remaining ¼ cup oil in a large bowl until smooth. Add the tomatoes, romaine, and onion; toss to coat. Divide the salad evenly among 4 plates; top with the steak. Sprinkle evenly with the chips and cheese.

CAMPFIRE-GRILLED BRUSSELS SPROUTS SALAD WITH BACON AND CIDER VINAIGRETTE

HANDS-ON: 20 MINUTES | **TOTAL:** 35 MINUTES | SERVES 4

The mustard mop on the Brussels sprouts allows for a more flavorful char and provides a tart, sweet balance to their natural flavor. Tossing with bacon, cider vinaigrette, and herbs rounds out this hearty salad.

2 tablespoons apple cider vinegar

2 teaspoons honey

1 teaspoon fresh lemon juice

½ cup olive oil, divided

1 teaspoon kosher salt, divided

1 tablespoon Dijon mustard

1 teaspoon minced garlic

¼ teaspoon black pepper

1 pound Brussels sprouts, trimmed and cut in half lengthwise

8 metal skewers

4 thick-cut bacon slices, cooked and crumbled

½ cup loosely packed fresh flat-leaf parsley leaves

1. Fit a grilling grate over the direct heat of glowing embers. Stir together the vinegar, honey, lemon juice, ¼ cup of the oil, and ½ teaspoon of the salt in a small bowl. Set aside.

2. Stir together the mustard, garlic, pepper, and remaining ¼ cup oil and ½ teaspoon salt.

3. Thread about 5 Brussels sprouts halves onto each skewer, spacing at least ½ inch apart. Brush the Brussels sprouts with the mustard mixture. Place the skewers on the grilling grate directly over the heat source, and grill until charred and tender, 6 to 7 minutes per side, brushing with the remaining mustard mixture about halfway through.

4. Remove the Brussels sprouts from the skewers, and toss with the crumbled bacon, parsley, and 2 to 3 tablespoons of the vinaigrette. Serve immediately with the remaining vinaigrette.

THINK LIKE A SCOUT

Hardy Brussels sprouts will fare much better on a camping trip than lettuce, making this an ideal salad to serve toward the end of the trip. They'll take up far less room in the cooler if you pluck them off the stem and halve them in advance.

CABBAGE, GRANNY SMITH APPLE, AND ASPARAGUS SALAD

HANDS-ON: 10 MINUTES | **TOTAL:** 20 MINUTES | SERVES 6

This refreshing, crunchy salad pairs perfectly with any grilled protein, like pork chops (as we've used here), steaks, or chicken.

½ cup olive oil
¼ cup apple cider vinegar
2 tablespoons honey
1 (1-ounce) package fresh basil, chopped
1 teaspoon kosher salt
1 pound fresh asparagus
1 large Granny Smith apple, cut into thin strips
1 (10-ounce) package finely shredded (angel hair) cabbage
1 bunch scallions, thinly sliced
Kosher salt and black pepper to taste

1. Whisk together the oil, vinegar, honey, basil, and salt in a small bowl.

2. Snap off and discard the tough ends of the asparagus. Cut the asparagus lengthwise into thin, ribbon-like strips, using a vegetable peeler. Toss together the asparagus, apple, cabbage, scallions, and dressing in a large bowl. Cover and chill 10 minutes. Add salt and pepper to taste just before serving.

MEXICAN STREET CORN SALAD

HANDS-ON: 15 MINUTES | **TOTAL:** 15 MINUTES | SERVES 8

This salad is fast, fresh, and so easy to make. The optional jalapeño will give it a wonderful kick, but feel free to omit or take it up a level with another hot chile pepper. Serve this alongside burgers, sandwiches, or tacos.

8 large ears fresh yellow corn, husks removed

3 tablespoons mayonnaise

½ teaspoon kosher salt

½ teaspoon black pepper

2½ ounces Cotija (fresh Mexican cheese) or feta cheese, crumbled (about ⅔ cup)

⅓ cup chopped fresh cilantro

¼ cup fresh lime juice (from 2 limes)

1 jalapeño chile, minced (optional)

1 lime

1. Heat a camping stove or grill to medium-high (about 375° to 400°F), or fit a grilling grate over the direct heat of glowing embers. Brush the corn evenly with the mayonnaise; sprinkle with the salt and black pepper. Grill the corn, turning occasionally, on the camping stove or grilling grate directly over the heat source until done, about 10 to 12 minutes. (Kernels may char and pop.)

2. Cut the kernels from the cobs into a large bowl. Add the cheese, cilantro, lime juice, and, if desired, jalapeño; stir to combine. Cut the lime into 8 wedges; serve with the corn salad.

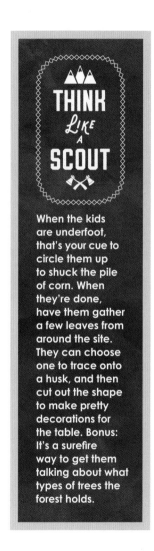

THINK Like A SCOUT

When the kids are underfoot, that's your cue to circle them up to shuck the pile of corn. When they're done, have them gather a few leaves from around the site. They can choose one to trace onto a husk, and then cut out the shape to make pretty decorations for the table. Bonus: It's a surefire way to get them talking about what types of trees the forest holds.

ZUCCHINI-AND-CARROT SLAW WITH HOMEMADE CATALINA DRESSING

HANDS-ON: 10 MINUTES | **TOTAL:** 40 MINUTES | SERVES 6

Instead of a traditional mayo-based dressing, try this homemade Catalina Dressing to sweeten the slaw.

1 pound zucchini
2 cups matchstick carrots
1 teaspoon kosher salt, divided
Catalina Dressing
¼ cup firmly packed fresh mint leaves, coarsely chopped
2 tablespoons thinly sliced fresh chives
½ teaspoon black pepper

1. Cut the zucchini lengthwise into ⅛- to ¼-inch-thick slices. Stack 2 or 3 slices on a cutting board, and cut lengthwise into thin strips. Repeat with the remaining zucchini slices.

2. Toss together the zucchini strips, carrots, and ½ teaspoon of the salt in a colander. Let stand 10 minutes to release water. Rinse with cold water, and pat dry.

3. Toss together the zucchini-and-carrot mixture and desired amount of Catalina Dressing in a large bowl; let stand 20 minutes, tossing occasionally. Sprinkle with the mint, chives, pepper, and remaining ½ teaspoon salt.

CATALINA DRESSING

HANDS-ON: 5 MINUTES | **TOTAL:** 5 MINUTES | MAKES 1½ CUPS

Whisk together ½ cup olive oil, ¼ cup granulated sugar, ¼ cup ketchup, ¼ cup red wine vinegar, ¼ cup grated sweet onion, ½ teaspoon paprika, ½ teaspoon Worcestershire sauce, ½ teaspoon hot sauce, ¼ teaspoon kosher salt, and ¼ teaspoon black pepper in a small bowl.

YOSEMITE VALLEY,
CALIFORNIA

GRILLED POTATO AND OKRA SALAD WITH HONEY-THYME VINAIGRETTE

HANDS-ON: 30 MINUTES | **TOTAL:** 55 MINUTES | SERVES 6

In this salad, slice the okra before grilling to decrease the slimy texture for which it can be known, or, if you like, use asparagus instead.

1 pound baby red potatoes
1 pound small Yukon Gold potatoes
1 pound fresh okra
2 tablespoons olive oil, divided
3 teaspoons kosher salt, divided
1 teaspoon black pepper, divided
3 scallions, thinly sliced
Honey-Thyme Vinaigrette

1. Heat a camping stove or grill to high (about 400° to 450°F). Place the potatoes in a large saucepan with water to cover; bring to a boil. Reduce the heat to medium-low (about 300° to 325°F); simmer until the potatoes are tender when pierced with a fork, 15 to 20 minutes. Drain and cool completely, about 20 minutes.

2. Cut the okra in half lengthwise. Toss together the okra, 1 tablespoon of the oil, 1 teaspoon of the salt, and ½ teaspoon of the pepper. Spread the okra mixture in a single layer in a jelly-roll pan. Cut the potatoes in half, and toss with the remaining 1 tablespoon oil, 2 teaspoons salt, and ½ teaspoon pepper.

3. Arrange the okra and potatoes in a single layer on the camping stove or grill. Grill, turning occasionally, until tender and slightly charred, 15 to 20 minutes. Remove from the grill; let stand 5 minutes.

4. Toss together the potatoes, okra, scallions, and Honey-Thyme Vinaigrette in a medium bowl.

HONEY-THYME VINAIGRETTE

HANDS-ON: 5 MINUTES | **TOTAL:** 15 MINUTES | MAKES ABOUT 1 CUP

Stir together 3 tablespoons white wine vinegar and 1 small minced shallot in a small bowl; let stand 10 minutes. Stir in 2 tablespoons honey, 1 teaspoon chopped fresh thyme, 1 teaspoon grated lemon zest, 2 tablespoons fresh lemon juice, and 1 teaspoon Dijon mustard. Add ¼ cup extra-virgin olive oil in a slow, steady stream, whisking constantly, until smooth.

PESTO EGG SALAD WITH ROMAINE HEARTS

HANDS-ON: 10 MINUTES | **TOTAL:** 10 MINUTES | SERVES 6

You can serve this easy egg salad on sandwich bread or rolls, if you like. Make the pesto ahead and store it in the fridge for up to a week.

2 cups firmly packed fresh basil leaves
2 ounces Parmesan cheese, grated (about ½ cup)
3 tablespoons extra-virgin olive oil
1 garlic clove, chopped
1 teaspoon fresh lemon juice
¾ teaspoon kosher salt, divided
8 hard-cooked large eggs, peeled and chopped
¼ cup mayonnaise
2 teaspoons Dijon mustard
¼ teaspoon black pepper
1 (5-ounce) package romaine lettuce hearts

1. Process the basil, Parmesan, oil, garlic, lemon juice, and ½ teaspoon of the salt in a food processor until finely ground. Refrigerate in an airtight container up to 1 week.

2. Stir together the eggs, mayonnaise, mustard, pepper, and remaining ¼ teaspoon salt in a medium bowl. Fold in the basil pesto. Spoon the egg salad into the romaine hearts.

TOASTED COUSCOUS AND VEGETABLE SALAD WITH LEMON-BUTTERMILK DRESSING

HANDS-ON: 25 MINUTES | **TOTAL:** 35 MINUTES | SERVES 6

You can serve this colorful, toasty salad either hot or cold.

DRESSING
¾ cup buttermilk
½ cup mayonnaise
3 tablespoons finely chopped fresh chives
1 tablespoon fresh lemon juice
1 garlic clove, smashed
½ teaspoon finely chopped fresh thyme
½ teaspoon kosher salt
½ teaspoon black pepper

COUSCOUS
1 tablespoon olive oil
1 cup uncooked pearl couscous
2 (3- x 1-inch) lemon peel strips
2 cups water
¼ teaspoon kosher salt

VEGETABLES
2 tablespoons olive oil
1 pound fresh asparagus, trimmed and cut into 2-inch pieces
1 red bell pepper, cut into 2-inch pieces
1 yellow bell pepper, cut into 2-inch pieces
1 small red onion, cut into 2-inch pieces
½ teaspoon kosher salt
¼ teaspoon black pepper

1. Prepare the dressing: Stir together all the ingredients in a small bowl. Cover and chill up to 2 days.

2. Prepare the couscous: Heat a camping stove or grill to medium (about 350° to 375°F). Heat the oil in a medium saucepan. Add the couscous and lemon peel strips; cook, stirring often, until golden, 7 to 8 minutes. Add the water and salt; bring to a boil. Cover and reduce heat to medium-low (about 300° to 325°F); simmer until barely tender, 8 to 10 minutes. Drain and discard lemon peel strips.

3. Prepare the vegetables: Heat the oil in a medium skillet over medium (about 350° to 375°F). Add the asparagus, bell peppers, onion, salt, and pepper. Cook, stirring occasionally, until tender, 12 to 15 minutes.

4. Toss together the couscous, vegetables, and ½ cup of the dressing. Drizzle the remaining dressing over the salad.

FARMINGTON RIVER,
CONNECTICUT

CHAPTER FOUR

HOT MAINS

LOADED MACARONI AND CHEESE BOWLS

HANDS-ON: 20 MINUTES | **TOTAL:** 30 MINUTES | SERVES 6

If you cook the pasta ahead, toss it with 1 tablespoon of canola oil and store it in a large ziplock plastic bag—this helps it from sticking together. For a vegetarian option, omit the sausage and chorizo.

2 tablespoons unsalted butter

6 ounces mild Italian pork sausage

1½ cups chopped red bell pepper (from 1 large pepper)

1½ cups chopped yellow onion (from 1 large onion)

4 ounces dry-cured Spanish chorizo, chopped (about ¾ cup)

5 tablespoons all-purpose flour

4 cups whole milk

8 ounces processed cheese (such as Velveeta), roughly chopped

4 ounces smoked mozzarella cheese, shredded (about 1 cup)

1 teaspoon table salt

½ teaspoon black pepper

1 (16-ounce) package large elbow macaroni, prepared according to package directions

1. Heat a camping stove or grill to medium-high (about 375° to 400°F), or fit a grilling grate over the direct heat of glowing embers.

2. Melt the butter in a cast-iron Dutch oven on the camping stove or grilling grate directly over the heat source. Add the sausage to the Dutch oven; cook, stirring to crumble, until browned, about 4 minutes. Add the bell pepper, onion, and chorizo, and cook, stirring often, until the vegetables are tender, about 5 minutes. Add the flour, and cook, stirring constantly, 1 minute. Slowly add the milk, whisking constantly. Cook, whisking constantly, until thickened, about 5 minutes. Remove from the heat. Stir in the cheeses, salt, and pepper, stirring until completely melted. Stir in the hot cooked pasta. Divide evenly among 6 serving bowls. Serve immediately.

THINK *Like* **A SCOUT**

When packing the cooler, remove the cardboard layer of any food packaging. It has a way of getting soggy and falling apart, leaving an unpleasant mess.

CHOPPED CUBAN RICE BOWLS

HANDS-ON: 30 MINUTES | **TOTAL:** 30 MINUTES | SERVES 4

This yummy and easy dish tastes like a Cuban sandwich in a bowl. Ask your local deli to slice a large chunk of ham for you.

2 tablespoons unsalted butter
8 ounces deli ham, chopped
1½ cups chopped yellow onion (from 1 large onion)
2 tablespoons chopped garlic
½ cup orange juice
⅓ cup chopped bread-and-butter pickles
1 tablespoon whole-grain mustard
1 (8- to 10-ounce) package yellow rice, prepared according
    to package directions
3 ounces Swiss cheese, shredded (about ¾ cup)
½ cup coarsely chopped fresh cilantro
½ cup chopped tomatoes (about 4 ounces plum tomatoes)
4 lime wedges

1. Heat a camping stove or grill to medium-high (about 375° to 400°F), or fit a grilling grate over the direct heat of glowing embers.

2. Melt the butter in a 12-inch cast-iron skillet on the camping stove or grilling grate directly over the heat source. Add the ham to the skillet, and cook, stirring occasionally, until browned, about 5 minutes. Add the onion and garlic, and cook, stirring occasionally, until the vegetables just start to soften, about 3 minutes. Add the orange juice, pickles, and mustard; cook until slightly reduced, about 4 minutes. Divide the hot cooked rice evenly among 4 serving bowls. Serve ham-vegetable mixture over rice. Sprinkle evenly with cheese, cilantro, and tomatoes. Serve with the lime wedges.

CHICKEN TORTILLA BOWLS

HANDS-ON: 15 MINUTES | **TOTAL:** 25 MINUTES | SERVES 6

Campfire nachos! Substitute pepper Jack cheese if you prefer your nachos a little spicy.

1 ripe avocado
⅓ cup sour cream
¾ teaspoon kosher salt, divided
2 tablespoons canola oil
6 ounces tortilla chips
8 ounces shredded boneless, skinless rotisserie chicken
4 ounces Monterey Jack cheese, shredded (about 1 cup)
¼ cup chopped scallions
1 jalapeño chile, sliced
¾ cup chopped tomatoes
¼ cup loosely packed fresh cilantro leaves (optional)

1. Place the avocado in a small bowl; mash with a fork until almost smooth. Stir in the sour cream and ¼ teaspoon of the salt; set aside.

2. Heat a camping stove or grill to medium (about 350° to 375°F), or fit a grilling grate over the direct heat of glowing embers.

3. Pour the oil into a 12-inch cast-iron skillet, and tilt to cover bottom completely. Spread the chips in the skillet. Sprinkle evenly with the chicken, cheese, scallions, jalapeño slices, and remaining ½ teaspoon salt. Cover with a lid or aluminum foil, and cook on the camping stove or grilling grate until the cheese is melted and the chicken is warmed through, 8 to 10 minutes. Dollop with the avocado mixture; sprinkle with the tomatoes and, if desired, the cilantro. Divide evenly among 6 serving bowls.

NORTH CASCADES
NATIONAL PARK,
WASHINGTON

CHEESEBURGER SOUP

HANDS-ON: 10 MINUTES | **TOTAL:** 25 MINUTES | SERVES 6

Be sure to toast the hamburger buns before cubing to keep them from getting soggy in this kid-friendly soup.

1 pound ground chuck
1 cup chopped yellow onion (from 1 large onion)
1 cup shredded carrots (about 5 ounces)
½ tablespoon chopped garlic
3 tablespoons all-purpose flour
1 teaspoon table salt
¾ teaspoon black pepper
3 cups beef stock
1 cup whole milk
12 ounces russet potatoes, peeled and cut into cubes
8 ounces sharp Cheddar cheese, shredded (about 2 cups)
2 toasted sesame seed hamburger buns, cubed (about 4 cups)

1. Heat a camping stove or grill to medium-high (about 375° to 400°F).

2. Heat a cast-iron Dutch oven on the camping stove or grilling grate. Add the beef; cook, stirring often, until the meat crumbles and is no longer pink, about 6 minutes. Remove the beef, and drain.

3. Add the onion, carrots, and garlic to the Dutch oven; cook, stirring often, until the onions are tender, about 7 minutes. Add the flour, salt, and pepper, and cook, stirring constantly, 1 minute. Add the stock, milk, and potatoes; bring to a simmer. Reduce the heat to medium (about 350° to 375°F), and simmer until the potatoes are tender, 5 to 7 minutes. Remove from the heat, and stir in the cheese and beef. Ladle the soup evenly into each of 6 bowls; top with the hamburger bun cubes.

THINK *Like A* SCOUT

Cover the cooked beef with an overturned plate or foil until you're ready to combine it with the other ingredients. Protein attracts bees, wasps, and yellow jackets in a hurry.

BLACK BEAN, CORN, AND FISH SOUP

HANDS-ON: 10 MINUTES | **TOTAL:** 20 MINUTES | SERVES 4

If you aren't a big fan of seafood, substitute shredded cooked chicken for the catfish.

2 tablespoons unsalted butter

1½ cups chopped red bell pepper (from 1 large pepper)

1 cup chopped celery (from 2 stalks)

3 tablespoons all-purpose flour

4 cups fish stock

1½ cups fresh or frozen corn kernels

1 cup drained and rinsed canned black beans

1 teaspoon kosher salt

1 pound catfish, cut into ¾-inch cubes

1 cup chopped tomatoes (from 1 medium tomato)

1 cup tortilla chips, roughly crumbled

4 lime wedges

1. Heat a camping stove or grill to medium-high (about 375° to 400°F), or fit a grilling grate over the direct heat of glowing embers.

2. Melt the butter in a cast-iron Dutch oven on the camping stove or grilling grate directly over the heat source. Add the pepper and celery to the Dutch oven; cook, stirring occasionally, until tender, about 6 minutes. Add the flour; cook 1 minute, stirring constantly. Add the stock, corn, beans, and salt; bring to a simmer. Cook 5 minutes, stirring occasionally.

3. Add the fish and tomatoes; cook, stirring often, until the fish is done, 6 to 8 minutes. Ladle evenly into each of 4 serving bowls. Sprinkle with the chips, and serve with the lime wedges.

THINK
Like
A
SCOUT

Always double-bag meat, cheese, and seafood—in this case fish—to keep them from contaminating the ice and other foods. Keep them well sealed for a fresh-smelling cooler.

SMOKY FISH STEW

HANDS-ON: 40 MINUTES | **TOTAL:** 40 MINUTES | SERVES 8

This one-pot meal is a warm, filling way to end a day spent outdoors. Adding the fish at the end of cooking ensures the pieces will stay whole.

2 tablespoons olive oil

1 cup chopped dry-cured Spanish chorizo (about 4 ounces)

1 cup chopped yellow onion (from 1 medium onion)

1½ teaspoons hot smoked Spanish paprika (pimentón picante)

2 (12-ounce) bottles lager beer

3 cups chicken broth

1½ teaspoons kosher salt

2 russet potatoes, cut into ½-inch pieces (about 4 cups)

3 ears corn, shucked and cut crosswise into 1-inch pieces or kernels removed (about 1½ cups)

4 ounces fresh green beans, cut into 1-inch pieces

1½ pounds grouper (or other white fish such as snapper, trout, cod, halibut), cubed

1. Heat a camping stove or grill to high (about 400° to 450°F), or fit a grilling grate over the direct heat of glowing embers.

2. Heat a large cast-iron Dutch oven on the camping stove or grilling grate directly over the heat source until hot, 5 to 10 minutes. Add the oil and chorizo, and cook, stirring often, until browned, about 4 minutes. Add the onion, and cook, stirring often, until softened, about 3 minutes. Add the paprika, and cook until fragrant, about 1 minute. Add the beer, and cook until slightly reduced, about 2 minutes. Add the broth and salt; bring to a boil. Add the potatoes; cook 5 minutes. Add the corn and green beans; cook until the potatoes are tender, about 3 minutes. Add the fish, and cook until cooked through, about 5 minutes. If using corn pieces, remove and serve on the side.

CAMPFIRE CREOLE GUMBO

HANDS-ON: 35 MINUTES | **TOTAL:** 45 MINUTES | SERVES 8

If you prefer shrimp, feel free to swap it in for the fish. Both are delicious in this tomato-based Creole classic.

2 tablespoons olive oil

1 pound pork andouille or other spicy sausage, cut into bite-sized pieces

2 (8-ounce) packages prechopped tomato, onion, and pepper mix

2 jalapeño chiles, sliced (about 3 ounces)

2 to 3 teaspoons Creole seasoning

1 (28-ounce) can peeled plum tomatoes, undrained

3 cups chicken stock

1 (12-ounce) bottle lager beer

3 cups chopped fresh okra (about 9½ ounces)

1½ pounds catfish or trout fillets, cubed

2 (8.8-ounce) pouches precooked long-grain white rice

Hot sauce (optional)

1. Heat a camping stove or grill to high (about 400° to 450°F).

2. Heat the oil in a large cast-iron Dutch oven on the camping stove or grill. Add the sausage, and cook, stirring occasionally, until browned, about 6 minutes. Add the vegetable mix and jalapeño, and cook, stirring often, until softened, about 5 minutes. Add the Creole seasoning; cook, stirring often, until fragrant, 1 minute. Slowly add the tomatoes, mashing them against the side of the Dutch oven as you add them. Stir in the stock and beer; bring to a boil, stirring often. Add the okra; reduce the heat to medium-low (about 300° to 325°F), and simmer, stirring occasionally, until the okra is tender, about 15 minutes. Stir in the fish and rice, and cook until the fish is cooked through and rice is tender, about 2 minutes. Ladle evenly into each of 8 serving bowls, and serve with the hot sauce, if desired.

THINK *Like* **A SCOUT**

Precooked pouches of rice are great options for campers since they're shelf-stable and already cooked, requiring you to simply warm them through once you're at the campsite. Embrace the convenience! Using them also leaves the stove's burners free for other jobs.

CHICKEN CHILE VERDE

HANDS-ON: 25 MINUTES | **TOTAL:** 25 MINUTES | SERVES 6

You can sub salsa verde for the green enchilada sauce. Serve with tortilla chips.

¼ cup olive oil

1 pound ground chicken

1 (8-ounce) package prechopped pepper, celery, and onion mix

2 poblano chiles, chopped (about 1½ cups)

1 teaspoon ground cumin

1 teaspoon dried oregano

4 cups chicken broth

1 (28-ounce) can hominy, drained and rinsed

1 (10-ounce) jar green enchilada sauce

½ teaspoon kosher salt

¼ teaspoon cayenne pepper

½ cup very thinly sliced radishes

4 ounces sharp Cheddar cheese, shredded (about 1 cup)

1. Heat a camping stove or grill to medium-high (about 375° to 400°F), or fit a grilling grate over the direct heat of glowing embers.

2. Heat the oil in a large cast-iron Dutch oven on the camping stove or grilling grate directly over the heat source until hot, about 5 minutes. Add the chicken; cook, stirring often, until the meat crumbles and is no longer pink, about 5 minutes. Add the vegetable mix, poblanos, cumin, and oregano, and cook, stirring occasionally, until soft, about 4 minutes. Add the broth, hominy, enchilada sauce, salt, and cayenne pepper. Bring to a boil, and simmer, stirring occasionally, until heated through, about 7 minutes. Ladle evenly into each of 6 serving bowls; top with radishes and cheese.

EASY CHEESY CORN CHIP CHILI

HANDS-ON: 25 MINUTES | **TOTAL:** 25 MINUTES | SERVES 6

The kids will love eating this smoky and rich chili straight out of the bag! For a little more heat, top with fresh jalapeño.

1 tablespoon unsalted butter
1 cup chopped yellow onion (from 1 medium onion)
1 cup chopped poblano chile (from 1 chile)
1 tablespoon sliced garlic
12 ounces ground chuck
1 tablespoon chili powder
1 tablespoon tomato paste
1 teaspoon table salt
2 (15-ounce) cans fire-roasted diced tomatoes, undrained
1 cup drained and rinsed canned black beans
½ cup water
6 (2-ounce) packages corn chips (such as Fritos)
3 ounces Cheddar cheese, shredded (about ¾ cup)
2 ripe avocados, coarsely chopped
Lime wedges (optional)

1. Heat a camping stove or grill to medium-high (about 375° to 400°F).

2. Melt the butter in a cast-iron Dutch oven on the camping stove or grilling grate. Add the onion, poblano chile, and garlic to the Dutch oven; cook, stirring occasionally, until softened, about 10 minutes. Add the beef; cook, stirring often, until the meat crumbles and is no longer pink, 5 minutes. Add the chili powder, tomato paste, and salt, and cook, stirring often, 1 minute. Add the tomatoes, beans, and water; bring to a boil. Cover, reduce the heat to medium-low (about 300° to 325°F), and simmer until slightly thickened, about 10 minutes.

3. Split open 1 side of each corn chip package; top the chips evenly with the chili, and sprinkle with the cheese and chopped avocado. Serve with lime wedges, if desired.

MUSTARD AND BROWN SUGAR–GLAZED STEAMED SALMON

HANDS-ON: 15 MINUTES | **TOTAL:** 45 MINUTES | SERVES 6

Impress the other campers with this simple but sophisticated dish. It's delicious with grilled asparagus, squash, zucchini, corn, or potatoes.

¼ cup coarse-grain Dijon mustard

¼ cup chopped fresh dill

2 tablespoons dark brown sugar

1 tablespoon minced garlic

1 teaspoon paprika

1 teaspoon kosher salt

1 teaspoon black pepper

1 (3-pound) skin-on salmon fillet

1 lemon, sliced (optional)

1. Fit a grilling grate over the direct heat of glowing embers. Combine the mustard, dill, brown sugar, garlic, paprika, salt, and pepper in a small bowl; spread the mixture evenly over the flesh side of the salmon. Place the salmon on a large piece of aluminum foil, skin side down; loosely wrap, and seal tightly.

2. Place on the grilling grate directly over the heat source, and cook until desired degree of doneness, 20 to 25 minutes. Let stand 5 minutes. Serve with the lemon slices, if desired.

THINK LIKE A SCOUT

If there's a nearby stream that's not too busy with humans, tuck a bottle of rosé or white wine into a calm eddy. Bringing it to the table, perfectly chilled and dripping with cold water, shows true camper's panache.

GRILLED SWORDFISH KEBABS

HANDS-ON: 45 MINUTES | **TOTAL:** 45 MINUTES | SERVES 4

Swordfish is perfect for skewers because it has a meatier quality than other fish and won't fall apart on the grill.

12 (12-inch) metal skewers
2 pounds swordfish fillets, cut into 32 (1-inch) cubes
1 large zucchini, cubed
1 large red onion, sliced into wedges
24 whole button mushrooms (about 1 pound)
24 cherry tomatoes (about 10 ounces)
16 lemon wedges (from 2 lemons)
4 ounces (½ cup) unsalted butter
5 garlic cloves, minced (about 1½ tablespoons)
¼ cup chopped fresh flat-leaf parsley
2 tablespoons fresh lemon juice
2 teaspoons kosher salt
1½ teaspoons black pepper

1. Fit a lightly oiled grilling grate over the direct heat of glowing embers.

2. Thread the skewers evenly with the swordfish cubes, zucchini slices, red onion wedges, mushrooms, tomatoes, and lemon wedges. Set aside.

3. Stir together the butter, garlic, parsley, lemon juice, salt, and pepper in a cast-iron skillet or saucepan. Place on the grilling grate directly over the heat source, and cook, stirring often, about 3 minutes.

4. Place the skewers on the grilling grate directly over the heat source, and grill until the fish is cooked through, 8 to 10 minutes, turning occasionally and basting with the butter mixture often. Remove the skewers from the grate, and brush with the butter mixture. Remove the grilled lemon wedges, and squeeze over the fish and vegetables.

THINK LIKE A SCOUT

Cap the ends of each skewer with a piece of fish or zucchini or a lemon wedge. Tomatoes and mushrooms have a way of slipping off before they are done.

CHIPOTLE CHILE–RUBBED WALLEYE

HANDS-ON: 15 MINUTES | **TOTAL:** 15 MINUTES | SERVES 4

This is a tasty, smoky meal that's quick to put together. Other hearty fish may be substituted for the walleye.

THINK *Like* **A SCOUT**

Premix the marinade and the spices for this and other recipes at home to help make campsite prep easier. Pack the spice mix in labeled ziplock bags or a small spice jar for ease.

1½ tablespoons olive oil
1 tablespoon minced chipotle chile in adobo sauce
1 tablespoon fresh lime juice
2 teaspoons minced garlic
1 teaspoon honey
¾ teaspoon kosher salt
¼ teaspoon ground cumin
¼ teaspoon onion powder
¼ teaspoon paprika
4 (6-ounce) walleye or catfish fillets

1. Heat a camping stove or grill to medium (about 350° to 375°F), or fit a grilling grate over the direct heat of glowing embers. Cut 4 (18-inch) squares of aluminum foil; coat one side with cooking spray. Combine the oil, chipotle chile, lime juice, garlic, honey, salt, cumin, onion powder, and paprika in a small bowl. Spread the mixture evenly over the fillets; place one fillet in the center on the greased side of each foil square. Bring the sides up and over the fillet; double-fold the top and sides of the foil to tightly seal.

2. Place the foil packets on the camping stove or grilling grate directly over the heat source, and cook until the fish is cooked through and flakes with a fork, about 8 minutes.

GARLIC-MARINATED STRIP STEAK

HANDS-ON: 30 MINUTES | **TOTAL:** 12 HOURS, 30 MINUTES | SERVES 4

Strip steak, otherwise known as a New York strip or top sirloin, comes from the short loin behind the ribs. Look for steaks with lots of fat marbling.

2 tablespoons olive oil
2 tablespoons minced shallots
1 tablespoon minced garlic
½ teaspoon table salt
½ teaspoon black pepper
1 (1½-pound) strip steak
¾ cup balsamic vinegar
1 tablespoon dark brown sugar
3 thyme sprigs

1. Combine the oil, shallots, garlic, salt, and pepper in a medium bowl; add the steak, and toss to coat.

2. Tear or cut 4 (18-inch) squares of heavy-duty aluminum foil. Cut the steak into 4 equal pieces. Place one steak piece in the center of each foil square. Drizzle with any remaining olive oil mixture. Bring the sides up and over the steak; double-fold the top and sides of the foil to tightly seal. Refrigerate 12 to 24 hours.

3. Heat a camping stove or grill to very high (about 450° to 500°F), or fit a grilling grate over the direct heat of glowing embers. Place the steak packets on the camping stove grate or grilling grate directly over the heat source, or place directly on the hot coals. Cook until desired degree of doneness, about 4 to 5 minutes per side.

4. Combine the vinegar, brown sugar, and thyme in a small saucepan on the camping stove or grilling grate. Bring to a boil, and cook, stirring occasionally, until the mixture is reduced to about ½ cup and thickened, about 20 minutes. Serve the sauce with the steaks.

INDIVIDUAL CAMPGROUND MEATLOAVES

HANDS-ON: 30 MINUTES | **TOTAL:** 50 MINUTES | SERVES 6

Making individual meatloaves cuts down significantly on the cook time, which is important when you have a bunch of hungry campers. To lighten your cooler, look for meatloaf mix, which is a combination of ground beef and pork.

2 tablespoons olive oil

1 (6-ounce) package prechopped yellow onions

1 (8-ounce) package sliced fresh mushrooms, finely chopped

1 tablespoon chopped fresh sage

1 pound ground beef

½ pound ground pork

½ cup fine, dried breadcrumbs

3 large eggs, lightly beaten

1½ teaspoons kosher salt

1 teaspoon black pepper

1 cup bottled barbecue sauce

½ cup chopped scallions (from 2 large scallions)

1. Heat a camping stove or grill to medium-high (about 375° to 400°F), or fit a grilling grate over the direct heat of glowing embers.

2. Heat the oil in a 12-inch cast-iron skillet on the camping stove or grilling grate directly over the heat source. Add the onions, mushrooms, and sage to the skillet, and cook, stirring occasionally, until browned, about 8 minutes. Place the mixture in a large bowl; cool.

3. Add the beef, pork, breadcrumbs, eggs, salt, and pepper to the bowl, and gently combine. Coat 6 (5¾- x 3¼-inch) mini loaf pans with cooking spray. Divide the mixture evenly among the loaf pans, and cook, covered, 10 minutes; coat each with the barbecue sauce. Cover and cook until a meat thermometer registers 145°F and the meat is no longer pink in the center, about 10 minutes. Carefully remove from the pans. Sprinkle each with the scallions.

BEEF JERKY HASH

HANDS-ON: 30 MINUTES | **TOTAL:** 35 MINUTES | SERVES 4

What a great use of beef jerky! This dinner will be a lifesaver on a day when the hike goes long or you can't pull yourselves away from the lake. Use your camping stove, and it will be ready in no time.

¼ cup olive oil
1 (20-ounce) package refrigerated diced potatoes with onions (such as Simply Potatoes)
1 red bell pepper, diced
1 cup finely chopped beef jerky (about 4¾ ounces)
½ cup bottled barbecue sauce
½ cup chopped scallions (from 2 large scallions)
¾ teaspoon black pepper
½ teaspoon kosher salt
2 tablespoons apple cider vinegar
Sour cream (optional)

1. Heat a camping stove or grill to high (about 400° to 450°F), or fit a grilling grate over the direct heat of glowing embers.

2. Heat a 12-inch cast-iron skillet on the camping stove or grilling grate directly over the heat source until hot, 5 to 10 minutes. Add the oil and diced potatoes, and cook, stirring often, until lightly browned, about 15 minutes. Stir in the bell pepper, and cook, stirring often, until the potatoes are tender, about 11 minutes. Stir in the beef jerky, barbecue sauce, scallions, pepper, and salt. Cook, stirring occasionally, until the mixture is heated through, about 3 minutes. Stir in the cider vinegar, and, if desired, top with the sour cream.

GETTING
GEARED UP

Cast-iron skillets are wonderfully versatile multi-use pans that you should have among your camping tools. They distribute heat evenly, are easy to clean, and last for generations. A Coleman® 10-inch cast-iron skillet is ideal for camping trips: It's large enough for multi-serving, one-pan dishes like this one, or to cook up smaller or individual servings when needed.

SPICY SAUSAGE-AND-PEPPER HOBO PACKETS

HANDS-ON: 20 MINUTES | **TOTAL:** 45 MINUTES | SERVES 4

Similar to Italian sub sandwiches, this easy meal can also be served in hot dog buns.

4 (4-ounce) spicy Italian sausages
1 large red onion, peeled and cut into 4 (½-inch-thick) slices
1 red bell pepper
1 yellow bell pepper
1 poblano chile
12 ounces baby red potatoes, quartered
¼ cup olive oil
4 teaspoons chopped fresh oregano
1 teaspoon kosher salt
1 teaspoon black pepper
Hot sauce

GETTING GEARED UP

Steam will pour out of a foil packet when you peel it open to check for doneness. Using tongs or a couple of forks will spare your fingers a scalding.

1. Fit a grilling grate over the direct heat of glowing embers. Arrange the sausages, onions, and peppers on the grilling grate, and grill until charred, about 10 minutes, turning occasionally. Remove from the heat. Slice the peppers.

2. Cut 4 (18-inch) squares of aluminum foil. Divide the charred sausages and vegetables evenly among the foil squares, placing in center; add the potatoes. Drizzle with the oil; sprinkle evenly with the oregano, salt, and pepper. Toss to coat. Bring the sides up and over the mixture; double-fold the top and sides of the foil to seal, making packets. Place the packets on the grilling grate directly over the heat source, and cook until the potatoes are tender, about 15 minutes. Open the packets, and add desired amount of hot sauce.

CHOPPED PEPPER, MOZZARELLA, AND PORK CASSEROLE

HANDS-ON: 15 MINUTES | **TOTAL:** 25 MINUTES | SERVES 4

Keep dirty dishes at bay with this one-pot meal. Serve with a lightly dressed green salad or steamed broccoli.

THINK LIKE A SCOUT

Double-bag and freeze the tenderloin, and it can easily last safely until the second or even third night of your trip. Meanwhile, it makes an extra ice block for the cooler.

2 tablespoons salted butter

1 (1-pound) pork tenderloin, trimmed and cut into ¾-inch cubes

1½ cups chopped red bell pepper (from 1 large pepper)

1½ cups chopped yellow onion (from 1 large onion)

1 tablespoon minced garlic (about 3 cloves)

**3 cups uncooked microwavable brown and wild rice
   [from 2 (8½-ounce) pouches]**

¾ cup chicken stock

1 teaspoon table salt

¾ teaspoon black pepper

4 ounces mozzarella cheese, shredded (about 1 cup)

¼ cup chopped fresh flat-leaf parsley

1. Heat a camping stove or grill to medium-high (about 375° to 400°F). Melt the butter in a 12-inch cast-iron skillet on the camping stove or grilling grate. Add the pork, and cook, stirring occasionally, until browned on all sides and cooked through, 6 to 8 minutes. Remove the pork from the skillet.

2. Add the bell pepper, onion, and garlic to the skillet; cook, stirring occasionally, 5 minutes. Add the rice, stock, salt, and pepper. Cover with foil; reduce the heat to medium-low (about 300° to 325°F), and cook until most of the chicken stock is absorbed, about 10 minutes. Return the pork to the skillet; stir in the cheese. Cook, uncovered, until the cheese is melted and the pork is heated through, 2 to 3 minutes. Sprinkle with the parsley.

CAST-IRON SKILLET GNOCCHI WITH PESTO

HANDS-ON: 10 MINUTES | **TOTAL:** 15 MINUTES | SERVES 4

Dumpling-like gnocchi, sold near the dried pastas, serves as the fortifying base for this skillet dish.

1 tablespoon salted butter
8 ounces pork sausage, casing removed
1 (16-ounce) package gnocchi
1 cup chopped scallions (about 1 bunch)
2 cups chopped tomatoes (about 2 small tomatoes)
½ cup chicken stock
3 tablespoons prepared pesto
1 (15-ounce) can cannellini beans, drained and rinsed
3 ounces Parmesan cheese, grated (about ¾ cup)
2 tablespoons chopped fresh flat-leaf parsley (optional)

1. Heat a camping stove to medium-high (about 375° to 400°F), or fit a grilling grate over the direct heat of glowing embers.

2. Melt the butter in a 12-inch cast-iron skillet on the camping stove or grilling grate directly over the heat source. Add the sausage to the skillet, and cook, stirring until the sausage crumbles and starts to brown, about 3 minutes. Push the sausage to one side of the skillet.

3. Add the gnocchi to the empty side of the skillet, and cook, stirring occasionally, until browned, about 4 minutes. Stir in the scallions, and cook until just starting to soften, about 1 minute. Stir the tomatoes, stock, pesto, and beans into the mixture in the skillet; cover and cook 4 minutes. Sprinkle with the cheese; cook, uncovered, until the liquid is thickened, the gnocchi is tender, and the cheese is melted, 1 to 2 minutes. Sprinkle with the parsley, if desired.

BOURBON-HONEY BABY BACK RIBS

HANDS-ON: 20 MINUTES | **TOTAL:** 1 HOUR, 50 MINUTES | SERVES 6

Take a lesson from your local barbecue joint and hand out hand wipes at the end of the meal. A cold water tap isn't going to cut it with these finger-lickin' ribs.

1 cup bourbon
½ cup honey
3 tablespoons apple cider vinegar
2 teaspoons black pepper
2 teaspoons onion powder
2 (3-pound) slabs pork baby back ribs
1 tablespoon kosher salt
¼ cup plus 1 tablespoon olive oil, divided

1. Heat a camping stove or grill to high (about 400° to 450°F).

2. Place the bourbon in a saucepan on the camping stove or grilling grate. Bring to a boil, and cook, stirring occasionally, until reduced to about ½ cup, 6 to 8 minutes. Stir in the honey, vinegar, pepper, and onion powder, and cook, stirring occasionally, until slightly syrupy, about 5 minutes. Remove the pan from the heat.

3. Reduce the heat to medium-low (about 300° to 325°F). Rub the ribs with the salt and ¼ cup of the oil. Wrap each slab separately in heavy-duty aluminum foil, wrapping tightly to form a packet. Place on grilling grate, and cook until the ribs are tender and done, about 1½ hours, turning the packets occasionally. Carefully remove from the grilling grate. Brush the grilling grate with the remaining 1 tablespoon oil, and increase the heat to medium-high (about 375° to 400°F). Remove the ribs from the foil, and arrange on the grilling grate. Cook, basting often with the bourbon sauce, until a crust forms on the outside of the ribs, about 2 minutes. Remove the ribs, and brush with the bourbon sauce. Cut the ribs between the bones, and serve with the remaining bourbon sauce.

THINK *Like a* SCOUT

Dispose of your trash bag promptly after a meal like this. The smell of the ribs will be irresistible to the forest's nocturnal scavengers.

TERIYAKI-GARLIC CHICKEN WINGS

HANDS-ON: 35 MINUTES | **TOTAL:** 35 MINUTES | SERVES 4

Serve over couscous for a hearty meal—or serve the wings on their own for a fun appetizer. The sauce may be made ahead.

⅓ cup soy sauce
3 tablespoons water
3 tablespoons rice wine vinegar
3 tablespoons dark brown sugar
2 tablespoons minced garlic
½ teaspoon kosher salt
½ teaspoon black pepper
1½ pounds chicken wings, separated at joints
1 tablespoon sesame seeds, toasted (optional)
Sliced scallions (optional)

1. Heat a camping stove or grill to medium-high (about 375° to 400°F), or fit a grilling grate over the direct heat of glowing embers. Stir together the soy sauce, water, vinegar, brown sugar, garlic, salt, and pepper in a small cast-iron skillet. Bring to a boil on the camping stove or grilling grate directly over the heat source. Cook until the mixture is reduced to about ½ cup and slightly thickened, about 10 minutes. Remove from the heat, and cool.

2. Combine ¼ cup of the soy sauce mixture and the wings in a bowl; toss to coat. Cut or tear 2 large pieces of aluminum foil. Place half of the wings in a single layer on one piece of foil. Bring the sides up and over the wings; double-fold the top and sides of the foil to tightly seal. Repeat the procedure with the remaining wings and piece of foil. Place the wings on the camping stove or grilling grate directly over the heat source. Cook, turning occasionally, until the chicken is done, 20 to 25 minutes. Remove the wings from the foil, and place directly on the grilling grate directly over the heat source; cook until golden brown, 2 to 3 minutes per side. Remove the wings, and drizzle with the remaining soy sauce mixture. Sprinkle with sesame seeds and sliced scallions, if desired.

THINK Like A SCOUT

This recipe will leave you a short stack of dishes but one very sticky grill or griddle. Set a pot of water to heat when you sit down to dinner, so you'll have warm water ready when the grill is cool and it's time to clean up. With a mess like this, you'll thank yourself for thinking ahead a bit.

SAGUARO LAKE,
ARIZONA

PORTOBELLO MUSHROOM QUESADILLAS

HANDS-ON: 25 MINUTES | **TOTAL:** 25 MINUTES | SERVES 6

Charring the vegetables before chopping gives these quesadillas a robust smoky flavor.

THINK LIKE A SCOUT

Grilling directly on your stove grate will make quite a mess, but grates can be removed and put into the dishwasher at home before the camp stove gets packed up for next time.

6 portobello mushroom caps, trimmed
1 red bell pepper, halved and seeded
1 large red onion, cut into ¾-inch-thick rings
Cooking spray
½ cup chopped fresh cilantro
1½ teaspoons kosher salt
1 teaspoon black pepper
6 (10-inch) flour tortillas
8 ounces Monterey Jack cheese, shredded (about 2 cups)
1 cup jarred salsa
1 cup sour cream
½ cup jarred pickled jalapeños

1. Heat a camping stove or grill to high (about 400° to 450°F).

2. Coat the vegetables with cooking spray. Arrange the mushrooms and bell peppers on the camping stove grate or grilling grate, and cook until charred and tender, about 8 minutes, turning once. Arrange the onions on the grate, and cook until charred and tender, about 12 minutes, turning once. Roughly chop the charred vegetables, and toss with the cilantro, salt, and pepper.

3. Reduce the heat to medium (about 350° to 375°F). Divide the vegetable mixture evenly among the tortillas, spooning on half of one side of each tortilla. Sprinkle each with about ⅓ cup cheese. Fold the tortilla over, and coat both sides with cooking spray. Carefully transfer the tortillas to the grate, and grill until the cheese is melted, 1 to 2 minutes per side. Cut into wedges, and serve with the salsa, sour cream, and jalapeños.

RATATOUILLE PIZZA

HANDS-ON: 30 MINUTES | **TOTAL:** 1 HOUR | SERVES 6

Fresh summer vegetables star in this simple grilled pizza recipe.
A sprinkle of fresh basil and red pepper flakes gives this pizza
an irresistible freshness.

1 pound fresh deli pizza dough
1 large zucchini (about 8 ounces), cut into ½-inch-thick slices
½ yellow squash (about 3½ ounces), cut into ½-inch-thick slices
½ medium-sized eggplant (about 8 ounces), peeled and cut into
    ½-inch-thick slices
¼ cup olive oil, divided
½ cup jarred pizza sauce
½ cup halved cherry tomatoes
6 ounces fresh mozzarella, cubed
¾ teaspoon red pepper flakes
½ teaspoon kosher salt
6 large fresh basil leaves, roughly chopped

1. Let the pizza dough stand unrefrigerated until pliable, 30 minutes to
1 hour. Heat a camping stove or grill to high (about 400° to 450°F). Coat the
grilling grate with cooking spray, and place on the camping stove or grill.

2. Brush the zucchini, yellow squash, and eggplant with 2 tablespoons of
the oil, and arrange on the grilling grate; grill the zucchini and squash
until charred, 3 to 4 minutes. Grill the eggplant until charred and tender,
6 to 8 minutes. Roughly chop the charred vegetables.

3. Reduce the heat to medium-high (about 375° to 400°F). Roll, pull, or
stretch the pizza dough to a 13-inch circle or 14- x 8-inch rectangle. Place
on the greased grilling grate; brush with 1 tablespoon of the olive oil. Grill
90 seconds, popping any bubbles that form on the surface. Turn and grill
90 seconds. Remove to a work surface. Spread the pizza sauce over the crust,
leaving a ½-inch border. Top with the grilled vegetables, tomatoes, and
cheese. Sprinkle with the pepper flakes and salt. Grill, covered, until the
cheese is bubbly, about 5 minutes. Sprinkle with the basil leaves, and brush
the edges with the remaining 1 tablespoon oil.

GETTING
GEARED UP

An oilcloth spread
on the picnic table
makes a nice big
work surface so the
pizza topping can
become a group
project. Just be sure
to wipe the oilcloth
down first with soapy
water in case critters
have walked over
it in the night.

ZUCCHINI, ONION, AND FETA FRITTATA

HANDS-ON: 20 MINUTES | **TOTAL:** 30 MINUTES | SERVES 6

At the end of the trip when all the meat has been eaten, this makes a quick, satisfying dinner.

¼ cup olive oil, divided
2 zucchini, cut into 1-inch-thick slices
1 cup chopped yellow onion (from 1 medium onion)
1 tablespoon chopped fresh oregano
8 large eggs, lightly beaten
¼ cup half-and-half
1 teaspoon kosher salt
1 teaspoon black pepper
4 ounces feta cheese, crumbled (about 1 cup)

1. Heat a camping stove or grill to high (about 400° to 450°F).

2. Heat 2 tablespoons of the oil in a 10-inch cast-iron skillet on the camping stove or grilling grate. Add the zucchini, onion, and oregano to the skillet, and cook, stirring often, until soft, about 6 minutes. Remove the skillet from the heat, and cool. Reduce the heat to medium (about 350° to 375°F). Combine the eggs, half-and-half, salt, and pepper in a bowl; stir in the grilled vegetables. Add the remaining 2 tablespoons oil to the skillet, and place on the camping stove or grilling grate until warm. Pour the egg mixture into the skillet; sprinkle the top with the feta. Cover with foil, and cook until the eggs are set, about 15 minutes. Remove from the heat, and let stand 10 minutes. Cut into 6 wedges, and serve immediately.

CHAPTER FIVE

SIDE DISHES

HONEY-GLAZED GRILLED FIGS

HANDS-ON: 10 MINUTES | **TOTAL:** 10 MINUTES | SERVES 4

This side dish will elevate your camping cuisine. The light char on the figs adds depth alongside the rich blue cheese and toasty walnuts. Serve it with grilled chicken, pork, or beef; it's also excellent as an appetizer. To hold up on the high heat of the grill, the figs need to be relatively firm, but not underripe. Mission figs are called for here, but you can use any variety you like.

1 tablespoon balsamic vinegar
1 tablespoon honey
¼ teaspoon kosher salt
⅛ teaspoon black pepper
1 pound firm, ripe Mission figs (about 8 large figs), halved
½ small navel orange (about 3 ounces)
1½ tablespoons olive oil
¼ cup chopped walnuts, toasted
2 ounces blue cheese, crumbled (about ½ cup)

1. Fit a grilling grate over the direct heat of glowing embers.

2. Whisk together the vinegar, honey, salt, and pepper until well combined.

3. Brush the cut sides of the figs and the cut side of the orange with the olive oil. Arrange the fig and orange halves, cut sides down, directly over the heat source, and grill until slightly charred, about 3 minutes. Remove the figs to a serving platter. Squeeze the juice from the orange half over the figs; drizzle with the vinegar mixture, and top with the walnuts and blue cheese.

SRIRACHA-LIME WATERMELON

HANDS-ON: 10 MINUTES | **TOTAL:** 10 MINUTES | SERVES 8

Make the seasoned salt ahead and store in an airtight container. Try sprinkling it over other melons, such as cantaloupe or honeydew. The wedges last well for several days with no cooling or babying required.

¼ cup kosher salt

1 tablespoon Sriracha chili sauce

1 tablespoon granulated sugar

2 teaspoons grated lime zest plus 3 tablespoons fresh lime juice (from 2 limes)

1 medium-sized watermelon (about 10 pounds), cut into wedges (about 1 inch thick)

1. Stir together the salt, Sriracha, sugar, and lime zest until well incorporated.

2. Drizzle the lime juice over the watermelon wedges; lightly sprinkle the wedges with the Sriracha-lime salt.

GETTING GEARED UP

Many people keep old, second-rate knives in their camping bin. But cutting into this melon is just one moment where you'll be glad you've brought a bona fide kitchen knife, like a Coleman® stainless steel carving knife. It will give you an excellent grip in addition to a sharp blade. Make a quick DIY sheath to protect it by folding thin cardboard over the blade, cutting it a half inch bigger than the blade, and stapling the cut edge.

PROSCIUTTO-WRAPPED ASPARAGUS WITH LEMON MAYO

HANDS-ON: 15 MINUTES | **TOTAL:** 15 MINUTES | SERVES 5

This dish may look fancy but it's simple to prepare at the campsite. Opt for medium to large asparagus spears, which are less likely to fall through the grate as they grill. The residual heat from the charred asparagus warms the prosciutto just enough after you've wrapped the bundles. The creamy lemon mayo sauce—a makeshift hollandaise—has just the right zing to contrast the richness of the prosciutto.

½ cup mayonnaise

1½ teaspoons lemon zest plus 2 tablespoons fresh juice
(from 1 large lemon)

1 tablespoon Dijon mustard

½ teaspoon black pepper

¾ teaspoon kosher salt, divided

2 pounds medium-sized asparagus spears (about 45), trimmed

2 tablespoons olive oil

6 ounces thinly sliced prosciutto (about 15 slices)

1. Fit a grilling grate over the direct heat of glowing embers.

2. Stir together the mayonnaise, lemon zest, juice, Dijon, pepper, and ¼ teaspoon of the salt until well combined. Set aside.

3. Brush the asparagus with the olive oil, and sprinkle with the remaining ½ teaspoon salt. Arrange on the grilling grate directly over the heat source, and grill, turning occasionally, until tender and lightly browned, about 3 minutes. Let cool slightly.

4. Wrap about 3 asparagus spears in each prosciutto slice, and serve with the lemon-mayonnaise mixture.

ROASTED BABY BELL PEPPERS

HANDS-ON: 10 MINUTES | **TOTAL:** 20 MINUTES | SERVES 4

We don't expect you to have any leftovers, but if you do, chop up any remaining peppers and add to your breakfast egg scramble.

1 pound baby bell peppers
4 (12-inch) flat metal skewers
2 tablespoons olive oil
¾ teaspoon kosher salt, divided
1 tablespoon balsamic glaze
2 ounces goat cheese, crumbled (about ½ cup)

1. Fit a grilling grate over the direct heat of glowing embers.

2. Thread 5 to 6 whole bell peppers onto each skewer. Drizzle evenly with the olive oil, and sprinkle with ½ teaspoon of the salt. Place the skewers on the grilling grate directly over the heat source, and grill, turning occasionally, until charred and tender, about 10 minutes. Remove the peppers from the skewers, and place on a serving plate.

3. Drizzle the peppers with the balsamic glaze. Sprinkle with the remaining ¼ teaspoon salt, and top with the crumbled goat cheese.

GETTING GEARED UP

Most campsites have a grate over the fire ring, but they can be rusty, with large gaps that smaller pieces of food can easily slip through. Bringing your own grate, one you cleaned yourself, can save you the frustration of food sticking or being lost to the fire.

SKILLET CHARRO BEANS

HANDS-ON: 15 MINUTES | **TOTAL:** 30 MINUTES | SERVES 6

Frijoles charros, also known as "cowboy beans," is a traditional Mexican dish made with pinto beans, bacon, garlic, and onions. It has a soupier consistency, so serve it with cornbread or a thick piece of bread to mop up the juice.

6 thick-cut bacon slices
1 cup chopped yellow onion (from 1 large onion)
2 garlic cloves, chopped
1 jalapeño chile, sliced
2 (15-ounce) cans pinto beans, drained and rinsed
1 (15-ounce) can fire-roasted diced tomatoes, undrained
1 cup chicken stock
½ cup lager beer
¾ teaspoon kosher salt
¼ teaspoon black pepper
½ cup chopped fresh cilantro

1. Heat a camping stove to medium (about 350° to 375°F), or fit a grilling grate over the direct heat of glowing embers.

2. Cook the bacon in a 12-inch cast-iron skillet on the camping stove or grilling grate directly over the heat source until crisp, about 8 minutes, turning once. Remove the bacon from the skillet, reserving the drippings in the skillet; crumble the bacon, and set aside. Add the onion and garlic to the hot drippings in the skillet, and cook, stirring often, until tender, about 6 minutes. Add the jalapeño, and cook until slightly tender, about 2 minutes.

3. Stir in the beans, tomatoes, chicken stock, beer, salt, pepper, and crumbled bacon. Cook, stirring occasionally, until slightly thickened, about 15 minutes. Stir in the cilantro, and serve immediately.

CREAMY PARMESAN BRUSSELS SPROUTS

HANDS-ON: 15 MINUTES | **TOTAL:** 20 MINUTES | SERVES 4

Just because you're in the woods doesn't mean you can't eat your veggies. This supereasy, creamy side is similar to a gratin or creamed spinach.

1 tablespoon olive oil
1 pound Brussels sprouts, halved
¼ teaspoon black pepper
¾ teaspoon kosher salt, divided
½ cup heavy cream
1 teaspoon chopped fresh rosemary
1 teaspoon finely chopped garlic
2 tablespoons grated Parmesan cheese, divided

1. Heat a camping stove to medium-high (about 375° to 400°F), or fit a grilling grate over the direct heat of glowing embers.

2. Heat the oil in a 12-inch cast-iron skillet on the camping stove or grilling grate directly over the heat source. Add the Brussels sprouts, pepper, and ½ teaspoon of the salt, and cook, stirring occasionally, until the Brussels sprouts are tender and golden brown, about 10 minutes.

3. Bring the heavy cream, rosemary, garlic, and remaining ¼ teaspoon salt to a simmer in a saucepan on the camping stove or grilling grate, and cook, stirring occasionally, until slightly thickened, about 8 minutes. Remove from the heat; stir in 1 tablespoon of the Parmesan cheese until melted.

4. Drizzle the sauce over the Brussels sprouts, and sprinkle with the remaining 1 tablespoon Parmesan cheese.

THINK LIKE A SCOUT

Halve the Brussels sprouts at home and pack them into an airtight container. This prep step will help the dish come together very quickly and will also save valuable cooler space.

APPALACHIAN
MOUNTAINS,
NORTH CAROLINA

SPICY SKILLET-ROASTED OKRA

HANDS-ON: 15 MINUTES | **TOTAL:** 15 MINUTES | SERVES 4

Keep the okra cut sides down to achieve a roasty char. Serve with any freshly caught fish. If you can't find Fresno chiles, substitute a jalapeño.

½ teaspoon ground cumin
½ teaspoon kosher salt
¼ teaspoon garlic powder
⅛ teaspoon cayenne pepper
1½ tablespoons olive oil
12 ounces fresh okra, cut in half lengthwise
1 red Fresno chile, seeds removed, sliced
½ tablespoon fresh lemon juice

1. Heat a camping stove to medium-high (about 375° to 400°F), or fit a grilling grate over the direct heat of glowing embers.

2. Stir together the cumin, salt, garlic powder, and cayenne pepper.

3. Heat the oil in a 12-inch cast-iron skillet on the camping stove or grilling grate directly over the heat source. Add the okra, cut sides down, and sprinkle the chile slices over top. Cook, undisturbed, until the bottom of the okra is golden brown, about 2 minutes. Stir the okra and chile slices, and cook, stirring occasionally, until the okra is tender, 4 to 6 minutes. Stir in the spice mixture, and cook, stirring constantly, until fragrant, about 30 seconds. Remove from the heat, and drizzle with the lemon juice.

TERIYAKI MUSHROOMS

HANDS-ON: 5 MINUTES | **TOTAL:** 20 MINUTES | SERVES 4

Feel free to substitute button mushrooms for cremini. Serve this earthy and rich dish over grilled steak, chicken, or burgers.

2 tablespoons salted butter
1 tablespoon olive oil
1 pound sliced cremini mushrooms
1 teaspoon chopped garlic
¼ cup teriyaki sauce
¼ cup dry sherry
¼ teaspoon red pepper flakes

1. Heat a camping stove to medium (about 350° to 375°F), or fit a grilling grate over the direct heat of glowing embers.

2. Heat the butter and olive oil in a 12-inch cast-iron skillet on the camping stove or grilling grate directly over the heat source. Add the mushrooms, and cook, stirring occasionally, until lightly browned, about 4 minutes. Add the garlic, and cook, stirring constantly, until fragrant, about 30 seconds. Stir in the teriyaki sauce, dry sherry, and red pepper flakes, and simmer until the mushrooms are tender and the sauce is slightly reduced, about 10 minutes.

THINK *Like* A SCOUT

Store mushrooms in a plastic bag in your cooler and they'll be slimy and inedible in no time. Mushrooms need to be dry, with plenty of airflow. You're better off keeping them in a paper bag outside the cooler, and using them early in the trip. Yes, they may dry out a bit, but they'll plump up during cooking.

GRILLED POTATO PACKETS

HANDS-ON: 15 MINUTES | **TOTAL:** 45 MINUTES | SERVES 4

Whether for breakfast, lunch, or dinner, these smoky, salty potatoes make for a great side dish. If you prefer peeled potatoes, have the kids wash their hands and earn their s'mores (peeling them right into the fire ring is fine!).

1 pound baby gold potatoes, halved
4 bacon slices, cooked and crumbled
2 tablespoons finely chopped fresh shallots
2 ounces (¼ cup) salted butter
1 teaspoon kosher salt
½ teaspoon black pepper
2 tablespoons chopped fresh parsley (optional)
Sour cream (optional)

1. Fit a grilling grate over the direct heat of glowing embers.

2. Cut 4 (12-inch) squares of aluminum foil. Divide the potatoes, bacon, shallots, butter, salt, and pepper evenly among the foil squares, placing in center. Bring the sides up and over the mixture; double-fold the top and sides of the foil to seal, making packets.

3. Place the packets on the grilling grate directly over the heat source, and cook until the potatoes are tender, 20 to 25 minutes. Remove from the grilling grate, and let stand 10 minutes before opening the packets. Sprinkle with the chopped parsley, and dollop with the sour cream, if desired.

THINK LIKE A SCOUT

When cooking with foil packets, you'll have better success if you use heavy-duty foil. Folding the edges tidily, instead of scrunching them, will keep juices inside. If you're worried about burning, putting a cabbage leaf below and above your ingredients acts as a shield against the heat of the coals. Finally, always put the packets on the coals, not directly on the flame, for effective, even cooking.

GRILLED SWEET POTATOES AND ZUCCHINI

HANDS-ON: 15 MINUTES | **TOTAL:** 30 MINUTES | SERVES 4

This versatile dressing has a balanced blend of tartness from the mustard and a slight sweetness from the honey. It pairs well with any seasonal vegetables you have on hand. Make sure to cut the veggies into even pieces so that they cook evenly on the grill. You can make the dressing ahead and store in an airtight container.

2 medium-sized sweet potatoes (about 20 ounces), peeled and cut into 1-inch wedges
2 small zucchini (about 10 ounces), cut into 1-inch slices
¼ cup olive oil, divided
¾ teaspoon kosher salt, divided
½ teaspoon black pepper, divided
1 tablespoon apple cider vinegar
2 teaspoons whole-grain mustard
1 teaspoon honey

1. Fit a grilling grate over the direct heat of glowing embers.

2. Toss together the sweet potatoes, zucchini, 2 tablespoons of the olive oil, ½ teaspoon of the salt, and ¼ teaspoon of the pepper. Arrange in a single layer on the grilling grate, and cook, turning occasionally, until slightly charred and cooked through, about 10 minutes for the zucchini and 15 minutes for the sweet potatoes. Transfer the cooked vegetables to a serving plate.

3. Whisk together the vinegar, mustard, honey, and the remaining 2 tablespoons olive oil and ¼ teaspoon each of the salt and pepper in a small bowl. Drizzle the dressing over the grilled vegetables.

SMASHED GARLIC BREAD

HANDS-ON: 10 MINUTES | **TOTAL:** 40 MINUTES | SERVES 4

Brushing the garlic butter on after grilling the bread ensures a crispy crust and a soft, pillowy, perfumed garlic center. This recipe will be tastiest early in the trip when the French bread is still fresh, though oiling and grilling it will help if it's gotten a bit hard.

1 garlic head
¼ cup olive oil, divided
2 ounces (¼ cup) salted butter, melted
2 tablespoons chopped fresh flat-leaf parsley
1 ounce Parmesan cheese, grated (about ¼ cup)
1 (12-inch) French bread loaf, halved lengthwise

1. Fit a grilling grate over the direct heat of glowing embers.

2. Cut off the pointed end of the garlic, about the top ½ inch, exposing the cloves. Place the garlic on a piece of aluminum foil, and drizzle with 1 tablespoon of the oil. Wrap tightly to seal. Place the foil packet on the grilling grate directly over the heat source, and grill until the garlic is soft, about 30 minutes.

3. Remove the garlic cloves, and place in a small bowl; smash the garlic, pressing with the back of a spoon to make a paste. Stir in the melted butter, parsley, and Parmesan cheese.

4. Brush the cut sides of the bread with the remaining 3 tablespoons olive oil, and place, cut sides down, on the grilling grate directly over the heat source. Grill the bread slices until crisp and lightly browned, 3 to 4 minutes. Turn the halves, and brush the cut sides evenly with the garlic-cheese mixture. Grill until the garlic-cheese mixture is melted, about 2 minutes. Cut each half into 2 pieces, and serve.

CREAMY STUFFED POTATOES

HANDS-ON: 10 MINUTES | **TOTAL:** 50 MINUTES | SERVES 4

Just like the ones you get at your favorite steakhouse, these stuffed potatoes go great with grilled steak or burgers. Start the fire (and put the butter out to soften) an hour ahead of time so you'll have a great bed of coals by the time you're ready to cook.

4 (6-ounce) Yukon Gold potatoes
2 tablespoons olive oil
2 teaspoons kosher salt
2 ounces (¼ cup) salted butter, softened
2 ounces mild Cheddar cheese, shredded (about ½ cup)
¼ cup sour cream
1 teaspoon ranch dressing mix (from 1 envelope)
1 tablespoon chopped fresh chives

1. Let the coals in a charcoal grill die down to partially glowing embers. Toss each potato with ½ tablespoon olive oil and ½ teaspoon salt. Wrap the potatoes individually with heavy-duty aluminum foil. Carefully bury the potatoes in the partially hot coals or embers, and let cook until tender, about 40 minutes, turning once.

2. Meanwhile, stir together the butter, cheese, sour cream, and ranch dressing mix.

3. Remove the potatoes from the ashes, and unwrap. Cut a slit down the center of each potato, and push the ends toward the center. Spoon about 2 tablespoons of the cheese mixture into each potato; sprinkle with the chopped chives.

BROCCOLI-CHEESE RICE

HANDS-ON: 5 MINUTES | **TOTAL:** 20 MINUTES | SERVES 4

Bring your grandmother's broccoli-cheese casserole to your campsite with this easy, kid-friendly version of the classic.

THINK *Like* **A SCOUT**

Get older kids involved in preparing this recipe. They'll love cutting the broccoli into florets (or "trees") with a pocketknife. The type with a locking blade is safest. If their knife safety passes muster, you could cut them loose on sharpening sticks for roasting marshmallows.

1 tablespoon olive oil
½ cup chopped yellow onion (from 1 small onion)
2 cups broccoli florets (about 6 ounces)
2 garlic cloves, chopped
½ cup chicken stock
½ teaspoon kosher salt
¼ teaspoon black pepper
1 (8.8-ounce) pouch precooked long-grain white rice
4 ounces mild Cheddar cheese, shredded (about 1 cup)

1. Heat a camping stove to medium (about 350° to 375°F), or fit a grilling grate over the direct heat of glowing embers.

2. Heat the oil in a 12-inch cast-iron skillet on the camping stove or grilling grate directly over the heat source. Add the onion, and cook, stirring occasionally, until tender, about 5 minutes. Add the broccoli, garlic, chicken stock, salt, and pepper; cover with a lid or aluminum foil, and cook until the broccoli is crisp-tender or tender, 5 to 7 minutes. Remove the lid, stir in the rice, and cook, stirring often, until the rice is heated through, about 4 minutes. Top with the cheese; cover and cook until the cheese is melted, about 4 minutes.

CHAPTER SIX

DESSERTS

S'MORES COOKIE CAKE

HANDS-ON: 10 MINUTES | **TOTAL:** 1 HOUR, 20 MINUTES | SERVES 10

This giant cookie is a sweet, indulgent treat that tastes like a traditional campfire s'more. The cookie base is soft and gooey when warm, but firms up after cooling. Bonus: Little kids will be spared a scorched marshmallow or burned fingers.

6 graham cracker sheets, divided
1 (17.5-ounce) package sugar cookie mix
4 ounces (½ cup) salted butter, softened
1 large egg, lightly beaten
1 (12-ounce) package milk chocolate chips
3 cups miniature marshmallows

1. Heat a camping stove to medium (about 350° to 375°F), or fit a grilling grate over the direct heat of glowing embers. Tear or cut 8 (12-inch) squares of aluminum foil. Crumple each foil square into a 2-inch ball. Flatten each slightly, and arrange on bottom of a 7½-quart cast-iron Dutch oven. Cover with the lid, and preheat on the camping stove or grilling grate directly over the heat source 10 minutes. Reduce the heat to medium-low (about 300° to 325°F).

2. Line the bottom and sides of a 9- x 2-inch round cake pan with 2 layers of aluminum foil, allowing the foil to extend about 1 inch above the rim of the cake pan. Fold the edges of the foil down to create an even ½-inch collar above the rim of the pan. Coat the foil with cooking spray.

3. Finely crush 4 graham crackers in a ziplock plastic freezer bag. Stir together the crushed graham crackers, cookie mix, butter, and egg until a soft dough forms. Press the dough into the prepared cake pan. Using tongs, lower the pan onto the foil balls in the Dutch oven. Cover and cook on the camping stove over medium-low until a knife inserted in the center comes out clean and the edges are golden, about 1 hour. Remove the Dutch oven from the heat.

4. Sprinkle the chocolate chips evenly over the top of the cookie in the Dutch oven; top evenly with the marshmallows. Cover with the lid, and let stand 10 minutes or until the chocolate melts and the marshmallows slightly soften. Coarsely crush the remaining 2 graham crackers, and sprinkle over the marshmallows. Lift the cookie out of cake pan using the foil collar as handles; cut into 10 wedges.

GETTING GEARED UP

With a Dutch oven and a roll of aluminum foil, you can make baked desserts you might not think would be doable on a camping trip. A 7½-quart cast-iron Dutch oven with a snug-fitting lid—Coleman makes one—is the most versatile.

GOOEY CHOCOLATE CHIP COOKIE WEDGES

HANDS-ON: 10 MINUTES | **TOTAL:** 1 HOUR, 55 MINUTES | SERVES 8

We guarantee this dessert will be a hit with kids and adults. The foil-lined pan makes for easy cleanup. Change up the mix-ins with your favorite nuts, chocolate, pretzels, or even peanut butter chips.

THINK *Like* A SCOUT

With this recipe's long cooking time, you may need to swap in a fresh propane canister before it's fully cooked. Be sure to pack a backup canister, and when you notice the flame on your stove dying out, turn it off completely, twist off the empty canister, twist on the new one, and then turn the stove back on. Store the empty canister in the open air and away from the fire.

6 tablespoons salted butter, melted
¼ cup whole milk
1 large egg
2 cups (about 8½ ounces) all-purpose flour
1 cup packed light brown sugar
1 cup semisweet chocolate chips
1 cup chopped pecans or walnuts
½ cup granulated sugar
½ teaspoon table salt
½ teaspoon baking powder
¼ teaspoon baking soda

1. Heat a camping stove to medium (about 350° to 375°F), or fit a grilling grate over the direct heat of glowing embers. Tear or cut 8 (12-inch) squares of aluminum foil. Crumple each foil square into a 2-inch ball. Flatten each slightly, and arrange on bottom of a 7½-quart cast-iron Dutch oven. Cover with the lid, and preheat on the camping stove or grilling grate directly over the heat source 10 minutes. Reduce the heat to medium-low (about 300° to 325°F).

2. Line the bottom and sides of a 9- x 2-inch round cake pan with 2 layers of aluminum foil, allowing the foil to extend about 1 inch above the rim of the cake pan. Fold the edges of the foil down to create an even ½-inch collar above the rim of the pan. Coat the foil with cooking spray.

3. Stir together the butter, milk, and egg in a bowl, stirring until well blended. Place the flour, brown sugar, chocolate chips, pecans, granulated sugar, salt, baking powder, and baking soda in a large ziplock plastic freezer bag; seal the bag, and toss to combine the ingredients. (This can be done ahead and brought with you.)

4. Add the milk mixture to bag; massage the ingredients until a dough forms, about 2 minutes. Turn the bag inside out to release the dough; press the dough into the bottom of the prepared pan. Using tongs, lower the pan onto the foil balls in the Dutch oven.

5. Cover and bake on the camping stove over medium-low until a knife inserted in the center comes out clean and the cookie is golden brown around edges, about 1½ hours. Remove the pan from the Dutch oven. Cool the cookie 15 minutes before cutting into 8 wedges.

BUTTERSCOTCH-PECAN BLONDIES

HANDS-ON: 15 MINUTES | **TOTAL:** 1 HOUR, 15 MINUTES | SERVES 8

These blonde brownies have a rich brown sugar base that's enhanced with butterscotch chips and toasted pecans. You can easily vary this recipe by substituting chocolate or cinnamon chips or using any type of nut you'd like.

9 tablespoons salted butter, melted, divided
2½ cups all-purpose baking mix (such as Bisquick)
1 cup uncooked regular rolled oats
¾ cup packed light brown sugar
½ cup granulated sugar
½ teaspoon table salt
½ cup whole milk
1 cup butterscotch chips
1 cup chopped toasted pecans

1. Heat a camping stove to medium (about 350° to 375°F), or fit a grilling grate over the direct heat of glowing embers. Cut 6 (18-inch) squares of aluminum foil; crumple each square into a 1½- to 2-inch ball. Arrange the foil balls on the bottom of a 7½-quart cast-iron Dutch oven; cover with the lid. Preheat on the camping stove or grilling grate directly over the heat source 10 minutes.

2. Meanwhile, line the bottom and sides of a 9-inch round cake pan with foil. Coat the foil on bottom of pan with 1 tablespoon of the melted butter.

3. Stir together the baking mix, oats, sugars, and salt in a large bowl. Add the milk and remaining 8 tablespoons melted butter to the baking mix mixture; stir until combined. Stir in the chips and pecans. Spoon the batter into the prepared cake pan, smoothing the top. Using tongs, lower the pan onto the foil balls in the preheated Dutch oven. Cover with the lid, and bake until a wooden pick or a fork inserted in the center comes out clean, 55 minutes to 1 hour and 5 minutes. Let cool. Cut into 8 wedges.

THINK *Like* **A SCOUT**

If you run out of light (or just need more) before finishing with dessert, strap a headlamp to a clear water bottle or white or clear plastic milk jug, with the light shining inward, and you've got an instant DIY lantern to finish up your prep and cleanup.

CINNAMON BISCUIT BITES WITH BROWN SUGAR–CARAMEL SAUCE

HANDS-ON: 20 MINUTES | **TOTAL:** 45 MINUTES | SERVES 6

Enjoy this sweet campfire twist on traditional monkey bread.

10 tablespoons salted butter, melted, divided
2 cups all-purpose baking mix (such as Bisquick)
1 large egg, lightly beaten
5 tablespoons granulated sugar, divided
2 teaspoons ground cinnamon, divided
½ cup whole milk, divided
¾ cup packed light brown sugar

1. Heat a camping stove to medium (about 350° to 375°F), or fit a grilling grate over the direct heat of glowing embers. Cut 6 (18-inch) squares of aluminum foil; crumple each square into a 1½- to 2-inch ball. Arrange the foil balls on the bottom of a 7½-quart cast-iron Dutch oven. Cover with the lid, and preheat on the camping stove or grilling grate directly over the heat source 10 minutes.

2. Meanwhile, grease a 9-inch round cake pan with 1 tablespoon of the melted butter. Stir together the baking mix, egg, 2 tablespoons of the granulated sugar, and 1½ teaspoons of the cinnamon in a bowl. Add 2 tablespoons of the melted butter and 6 tablespoons of the milk; stir until a soft dough forms. Combine the remaining 3 tablespoons granulated sugar and ½ teaspoon cinnamon on a plate. Shape the dough into balls, using about 1 heaping tablespoon of dough for each. Roll in the sugar mixture on plate, coating all sides. Place the coated dough balls in the prepared cake pan.

3. Using tongs, lower the greased cake pan onto the foil balls in the preheated Dutch oven. Cover with the lid, and bake until the biscuit bites are done, 25 to 30 minutes.

4. Stir together the brown sugar, remaining 7 tablespoons butter, and remaining 2 tablespoons milk in a saucepan. Bring to a boil on the camping stove or grilling grate, and cook, stirring constantly, 2 minutes. Serve the warm sauce with the biscuit bites.

THINK *Like* **A SCOUT**

Many of these dessert recipes use a technique of cooking on top of balled-up aluminum foil. The bonus is, after they cool, the balls of foil can be handed to the kids to sculpt into animal shapes, toss at a pyramid of empty food cans, or flatten out to decorate with colored markers. It may buy you a few extra minutes to make breakfast in the morning.

SALTED CARAMEL–MARSHMALLOW BAKED APPLES

HANDS-ON: 10 MINUTES | **TOTAL:** 1 HOUR, 25 MINUTES | SERVES 8

No plate required! Dive straight into these buttery, luscious, and sweet apples. For an extraspecial touch, sprinkle the apples with ground cinnamon.

8 large Fuji apples (about 4¼ pounds), cored
1 teaspoon table salt
1 cup miniature marshmallows
16 caramels
4 ounces (½ cup) salted butter

1. Heat a camping stove to medium (about 350° to 375°F), or fit a grilling grate over the direct heat of glowing embers. Tear or cut 16 (12-inch) squares of aluminum foil. Crumple each of 8 foil squares into a 2-inch ball; flatten slightly, and arrange on the bottom of a 7½-quart cast-iron Dutch oven. Cover with the lid, and preheat on the camping stove or on the grilling grate directly over the heat source 10 minutes. Reduce the heat to medium-low (about 300° to 325°F).

2. Place the remaining 8 squares of foil flat on a work surface. Place 1 apple in the center of each square; sprinkle the inside of the hollow core of each apple with ⅛ teaspoon salt. Press 4 to 5 marshmallows and 2 caramel candies into each apple, and fill with the remaining mini marshmallows. Place 1 tablespoon butter on the top of each apple. Bring the corners of the foil up and over the top of each apple, and wrap tightly to seal (to prevent juices from leaking out).

3. Place one foil-wrapped apple on each ball in the Dutch oven. Cover and cook on the camping stove over medium-low until the apples are tender, about 1 hour and 15 minutes.

APPLE CRISP

HANDS-ON: 10 MINUTES │ **TOTAL:** 1 HOUR, 15 MINUTES │ SERVES 6

Any kids who have shown they've got their knife skills down can be put to work peeling and slicing the apples to make the prep a snap. Kids love using pocketknives—those with a blade that locks into place are safest.

2 ounces (¼ cup) salted butter

4 pounds Fuji apples (about 7 large), peeled, cut into ½-inch slices

1 cup apple juice

½ cup (about 2⅛ ounces) all-purpose flour

½ cup granulated sugar

½ cup packed light brown sugar

1 teaspoon ground cinnamon

½ teaspoon table salt

2 cups premium granola without fruit

1. Heat a camping stove to medium (about 350° to 375°F), or fit a grilling grate over the direct heat of glowing embers. Melt the butter in a 7½-quart cast-iron Dutch oven on the camping stove. Add the apples, apple juice, flour, granulated sugar, brown sugar, cinnamon, and salt to the Dutch oven. Stir well to coat the apples, and cook until the sugars melt and the mixture is thoroughly heated, about 5 minutes. Reduce the heat to medium-low (about 300° to 325°F).

2. Cover with the lid, and cook until the apples are tender, about 1 hour, stirring often to prevent the bottom from burning. Remove from the heat, and sprinkle with the granola.

MIXED BERRY COBBLER

HANDS-ON: 10 MINUTES | **TOTAL:** 40 MINUTES | SERVES 8

Berry-licious! The flavors of strawberry and blueberry stay distinct if you don't stir the fillings together. Pour cold whipping cream over the top when it's piping hot for a creamy contrast.

4 ounces (½ cup) salted butter, melted and divided
1 (21-ounce) can strawberry pie filling
1 (21-ounce) can blueberry pie filling
2 cups all-purpose baking mix (such as Bisquick)
¼ cup granulated sugar
¼ cup whole milk
Cinnamon-sugar (optional)

1. Heat a camping stove to medium (about 350° to 375°F). Pour ¼ cup of the melted butter in a 7½-quart cast-iron Dutch oven, and place on the camping stove. Add the strawberry pie filling; top with the blueberry pie filling. (Do not stir the pie fillings together.) Bring to a simmer.

2. Combine the baking mix, sugar, milk, and the remaining ¼ cup melted butter in a bowl; stir until a dough forms. Crumble the dough evenly over the simmering fruit in the Dutch oven; reduce the heat to medium-low (about 300° to 325°F).

3. Cover the Dutch oven with the lid, and cook until the topping is set, about 30 minutes. Sprinkle with the cinnamon-sugar, if desired.

PAINTED HILLS,
OREGON

CARAMELIZED PEACH COBBLER

HANDS-ON: 20 MINUTES | **TOTAL:** 1 HOUR | SERVES 8

Sweet, tender peaches beneath a cakey cobbler topping will warm the heart. The cinnamon-sugar topping adds a sweet crunch to this steamed dessert.

1 cup packed light brown sugar
8 ounces (1 cup) salted butter, divided
3 (23.5-ounce) jars sliced peaches in juice, drained
2 cups all-purpose baking mix (such as Bisquick)
1 cup granulated sugar
½ cup whole milk
2 large eggs, lightly beaten
Cinnamon-sugar (optional)

1. Heat a camping stove to medium (about 350° to 375°F). Place the brown sugar and ¾ cup of the butter in a 7½-quart cast-iron Dutch oven. Place on camping stove, and cook, stirring often, until the brown sugar and butter are melted and well combined, about 4 minutes. Increase the camping stove heat to medium-high (about 375° to 400°F). Add the drained peaches to the Dutch oven, and bring the mixture to a boil, stirring occasionally. Return the heat to medium, and cook, stirring occasionally, until the peaches are slightly softened, about 5 minutes.

2. Stir together the baking mix and granulated sugar in a medium bowl. Melt the remaining ¼ cup butter, and add to the baking mix mixture with the milk and eggs. Stir the mixture until well combined (a few lumps may remain). Pour the batter evenly over the peach mixture in the Dutch oven. (The peach mixture will bubble up into the batter.) Cover with the lid; reduce the heat to medium-low (about 300° to 325°F), and cook until a knife inserted in the center of the topping comes out clean, 25 to 30 minutes. Cool 10 minutes before serving. Sprinkle with the cinnamon-sugar, if desired.

BANANA PUDDING CAKE

HANDS-ON: 10 MINUTES | **TOTAL:** 55 MINUTES | SERVES 8

Bananas will ripen quickly in a hot car or bear box. Plan on serving this cakey twist on banana cream pie early in your trip—or buy the bananas green.

1 (15.25-ounce) box yellow cake mix
1 cup lemon-lime soft drink (such as Sprite)
4 ounces (½ cup) salted butter, melted
1 (3.4-ounce) box banana cream instant pudding mix
2 cups evaporated milk
3 medium-sized bananas, cut into ¼-inch slices (about 2½ cups)

1. Heat a camping stove to medium-high (about 375° to 400°F), or fit a grilling grate over the direct heat of glowing embers. Tear or cut 8 (12-inch) squares of aluminum foil. Crumple each foil square into a 2-inch ball. Flatten each ball slightly, and arrange on the bottom of a 7½-quart cast-iron Dutch oven. Cover with the lid, and preheat the Dutch oven 10 minutes. Reduce the heat to medium (about 350° to 375°F).

2. Line the bottom and sides of a 9- x 2-inch round cake pan with 2 layers of aluminum foil, allowing the foil to extend about 1 inch above the rim of the cake pan. Fold the edges of the foil down to create an even ½-inch collar above the rim of the pan. Coat the foil with cooking spray.

3. Whisk together the cake mix, soft drink, and butter in a bowl until well combined. Pour the mixture into the prepared cake pan. Using tongs, lower the pan onto the foil balls in the Dutch oven. Cover and bake on the camping stove over medium until a wooden pick inserted in the center comes out clean, about 40 minutes. Remove the cake pan from the Dutch oven.

4. Whisk together the pudding and milk in a medium bowl until thick and creamy, about 2 minutes. Gently fold in the bananas. To serve, spoon the pudding mixture evenly over the cake servings.

THINK *Like A* **SCOUT**

If you bring a 2-liter plastic bottle of lemon-lime soda, the last of it can come in handy if wasps or yellow jackets are around. Cut off the top third of the bottle. Put an inch or so of soda (to attract the bugs) and a couple drops of dish soap (to trap them) into the bottom part of the bottle. Place the top part upside down into the bottom part and set your contraption a little bit away from your picnic table.

GOOEY CHERRY-CHOCOLATE CAKE

HANDS-ON: 10 MINUTES | **TOTAL:** 1 HOUR | SERVES 10

Decadent and chocolaty, this dessert also goes easy on the cooler, with a bit of butter the only ingredient that needs to be kept cool. It's a big win for the last night of a campout.

1 (15.25-ounce) box dark chocolate cake mix
1 cup spicy, fruity cola soft drink (such as Dr Pepper)
2 ounces (¼ cup) salted butter, melted
1 (21-ounce) can cherry pie filling

1. Heat a camping stove to medium-high (about 375° to 400°F), or fit a grilling grate over the direct heat of glowing embers. Tear or cut 8 (12-inch) squares of aluminum foil. Crumple each foil square into a 2-inch ball. Flatten each slightly, and arrange on the bottom of a 7½-quart cast-iron Dutch oven. Cover with the lid, and preheat on the camping stove or grilling grate directly over the heat source 10 minutes. Reduce the heat to medium (about 350° to 375°F).

2. Line the bottom and sides of a 9- x 3-inch springform pan with 2 layers of foil, allowing the foil to extend about 1 inch above the rim of the pan. Fold the edges of the foil down to create an even ½-inch collar above the rim of the pan. Coat the foil with cooking spray.

3. Whisk together the cake mix, cola soft drink, and butter in a bowl until well blended. Gently stir in the pie filling. Pour the mixture into the prepared springform pan. Using tongs, lower the pan onto the foil balls in the Dutch oven. Cover and bake on the camping stove over medium until a wooden pick inserted in the center comes out with moist crumbs attached, about 45 minutes.

TRES LECHES CAKE

HANDS-ON: 10 MINUTES | **TOTAL:** 1 HOUR, 10 MINUTES | SERVES 8

Tres leches, or "three milks," cake is popular in Central and South America. No one will be expecting it on a camping trip, but its oozing sweetness will be irresistible. Be sure to pour the last two milks on while the cake is still warm, and serve it right away.

1 (15.25-ounce) box vanilla cake mix
¾ cup whole milk
4 ounces (½ cup) salted butter, melted
1½ teaspoons ground cinnamon, divided
½ cup sweetened condensed milk
1 (5-ounce) can evaporated milk
2 tablespoons powdered sugar

1. Heat a camping stove to medium-high (about 375° to 400°F), or fit a grilling grate over the direct heat of glowing embers. Tear or cut 8 (12-inch) squares of aluminum foil. Crumple each foil square into a 2-inch ball. Flatten each slightly, and arrange on the bottom of a 7½-quart cast-iron Dutch oven. Cover with the lid, and preheat on the camping stove or grilling grate directly over the heat source 10 minutes. Reduce the heat to medium (about 350° to 375°F).

2. Line the bottom and sides of a 9- x 2-inch round cake pan with 2 layers of aluminum foil, allowing the foil to extend about 1 inch above the rim of the cake pan. Fold the edges of the foil down to create an even ½-inch collar above the rim of the pan. Coat the foil with cooking spray.

3. Whisk together the cake mix, whole milk, butter, and 1 teaspoon of the cinnamon in a bowl until blended. Pour the mixture into the prepared cake pan. Using tongs, lower the pan onto the foil balls in the Dutch oven. Cover and cook on the camping stove over medium until a wooden pick inserted in the center comes out clean, about 35 minutes. Remove the cake pan from the Dutch oven; cool 20 minutes.

4. Poke holes all over the top of the cake using a skewer or a fork. Stir together the condensed milk and evaporated milk; gradually pour mixture over the cake, tilting the cake pan so that the milk mixture soaks in evenly. Combine the powdered sugar and the remaining ½ teaspoon cinnamon; sprinkle over the top of the cake. Cut into 8 wedges. Serve warm.

PINEAPPLE CELEBRATION CAKE

HANDS-ON: 10 MINUTES | **TOTAL:** 55 MINUTES | SERVES 8

Whether you're celebrating a successful morning of fishing or bagging a nearby peak, this will be a welcome reward at the end of a big day.

1 (15.25-ounce) box confetti cake mix
2 (8-ounce) cans crushed pineapple, drained
1 cup lemon-lime soft drink (such as Sprite)
4 ounces (½ cup) salted butter, melted

1. Heat a camping stove to medium-high (about 375° to 400°F), or fit a grilling grate over the direct heat of glowing embers. Tear or cut 8 (12-inch) squares of aluminum foil. Crumple each foil square into a 2-inch ball. Flatten each foil ball slightly, and arrange on the bottom of a 7½-quart cast-iron Dutch oven. Cover with the lid, and preheat on the camping stove or grilling grate directly over the heat source 10 minutes. Reduce the heat to medium (about 350° to 375°F).

2. Line the bottom and sides of a 9- x 2-inch round cake pan with 2 layers of aluminum foil, allowing the foil to extend about 1 inch above the rim of the cake pan. Fold the edges of the foil down to create an even ½-inch collar above the rim of the pan. Coat the foil with cooking spray.

3. Whisk together the cake mix, pineapple, soft drink, and butter in a bowl until well combined. Pour the batter into the prepared cake pan. Using tongs, lower the cake pan onto the foil balls in the Dutch oven. Cover and bake on the camping stove over medium until a wooden pick inserted in the center comes out clean, about 40 minutes. Spoon into each of 8 shallow bowls to serve warm, or cool completely, and cut into 8 wedges.

MOCHA TOFFEE CAKE

HANDS-ON: 10 MINUTES | **TOTAL:** 45 MINUTES | SERVES 8

Brew an extra cup of coffee in the morning, and this will be your after-dinner reward.

1 (15.25-ounce) box chocolate fudge cake mix
1 cup prepared strong coffee, at room temperature
4 ounces (½ cup) salted butter, melted
5 (1.4-ounce) chocolate-covered toffee candy bars (such as
    Heath or Skor), divided
Caramel topping (optional)

1. Heat a camping stove to medium-high (about 375° to 400°F), or fit a grilling grate over the direct heat of glowing embers. Tear or cut 8 (12-inch) squares of aluminum foil. Crumple each foil square into a 2-inch ball. Flatten each foil ball slightly, and arrange on the bottom of a 7½-quart cast-iron Dutch oven. Cover with the lid, and preheat the Dutch oven 10 minutes. Reduce the heat to medium (about 350° to 375°F).

2. Line the bottom and sides of a 9- x 2-inch round cake pan with 2 layers of aluminum foil, allowing the foil to extend about 1 inch above the rim of the cake pan. Fold the edges of the foil down to create an even ½-inch collar above the rim of the pan. Coat the foil with cooking spray.

3. Whisk together the cake mix, coffee, and butter in a bowl until well combined. Pour the mixture into the prepared cake pan. Break 3 of the candy bars into 1-inch pieces; top the batter with candy pieces. Using tongs, lower the cake pan onto the foil balls in the Dutch oven.

4. Cover and bake on the camping stove over medium until a wooden pick inserted in the center comes out clean, about 30 minutes. Remove the pan from the Dutch oven. Chop the remaining 2 candy bars; sprinkle over the top of the cake. To serve warm, spoon into each of 8 bowls, and drizzle with the caramel topping, if desired, or cool completely and slice.

METRIC EQUIVALENTS

The recipes that appear in this cookbook use the standard United States method for measuring liquid and dry or solid ingredients (teaspoons, tablespoons, and cups). The information in the following charts is provided to help cooks outside the U.S. successfully use these recipes. All equivalents are approximate.

Metric Equivalents for Different Types of Ingredients

A standard cup measure of a dry or solid ingredient will vary in weight depending on the type of ingredient. A standard cup of liquid is the same volume for any type of liquid. Use the following chart when converting standard cup measures to grams (weight) or milliliters (volume).

Standard Cup	Fine Powder (ex. flour)	Grain (ex. rice)	Granular (ex. sugar)	Liquid Solids (ex. butter)	Liquid (ex. milk)
1	140 g	150 g	190 g	200 g	240 ml
¾	105 g	113 g	143 g	150 g	180 ml
⅔	93 g	100 g	125 g	133 g	160 ml
½	70 g	75 g	95 g	100 g	120 ml
⅓	47 g	50 g	63 g	67 g	80 ml
¼	35 g	38 g	48 g	50 g	60 ml
⅛	18 g	19 g	24 g	25 g	30 ml

Useful Equivalents for Liquid Ingredients by Volume

¼ tsp					=	1 ml
½ tsp					=	2 ml
1 tsp					=	5 ml
3 tsp	=	1 Tbsp	=	=	½ fl oz	=	15 ml
		2 Tbsp	=	⅛ cup	1 fl oz	=	30 ml
		4 Tbsp	=	¼ cup	2 fl oz	=	60 ml
		5 ⅓ Tbsp	=	⅓ cup	3 fl oz	=	80 ml
		8 Tbsp	=	½ cup	4 fl oz	=	120 ml
		10 ⅔ Tbsp	=	⅔ cup	5 fl oz	=	160 ml
		12 Tbsp	=	¾ cup	6 fl oz	=	180 ml
		16 Tbsp	=	1 cup	8 fl oz	=	240 ml
		1 pt	=	2 cups	16 fl oz	=	480 ml
		1 qt	=	4 cups	32 fl oz	=	960 ml
					33 fl oz	=	1000 ml	= 1 l

Useful Equivalents for Dry Ingredients by Weight

(To convert ounces to grams, multiply the number of ounces by 30.)

1 oz	=	1/16 lb	=	30 g
4 oz	=	¼ lb	=	120 g
8 oz	=	½ lb	=	240 g
12 oz	=	¾ lb	=	360 g
16 oz	=	1 lb	=	480 g

Useful Equivalents for Length

(To convert inches to centimeters, multiply the number of inches by 2.5.)

1 in			=	2.5 cm		
6 in	=	½ ft	=	15 cm		
12 in	=	1 ft	=	30 cm		
36 in	=	3 ft	1 yd	=	90 cm		
40 in			=	100 cm	=	1 m

Useful Equivalents for Cooking/Oven Temperatures

	Fahrenheit	Celsius	Gas Mark
Freeze Water	32° F	0° C	
Room Temperature	68° F	20° C	
Boil Water	212° F	100° C	
Bake	325° F	160° C	3
	350° F	180° C	4
	375° F	190° C	5
	400° F	200° C	6
	425° F	220° C	7
	450° F	230° C	8
Broil			Grill

PHOTOGRAPHY CREDITS

INDEX